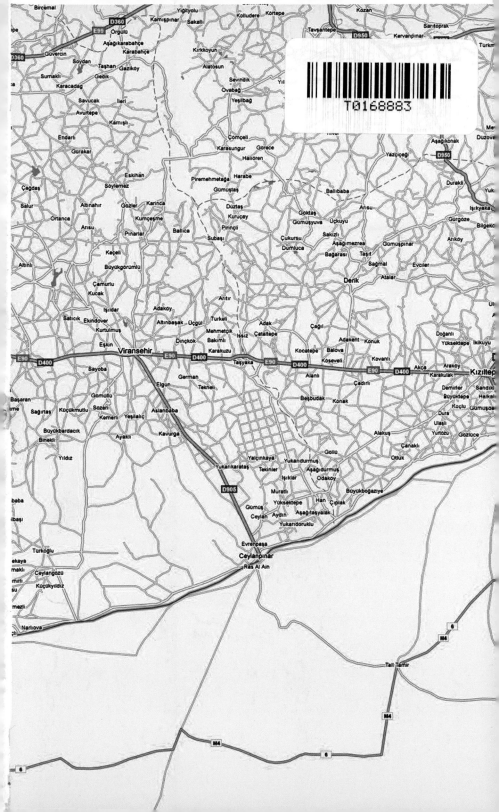

Şanlıurfa

City Guide

Adem Akıncı

TUGHRA
BOOKS

New Jersey

Published by Tughra Books
345 Clifton Ave., Clifton,
NJ, 07011, USA

www.tughrabooks.com

Edited by Hasan Hayri Demirel, Korkut Altay

Translated from Turkish by Nagihan Haliloğlu

Copy Editors Jane Louise Kandur, Ruth Woodhall

Art Director Engin Çiftçi

Graphic Design Sinan Özdemir, Erhan Kara

Photographs Ahmet Cihat Kürkçüoğlu

ISBN: 978-1-59784-207-5

Printed by
Çağlayan A.Ş., Izmir - Turkey

CONTENTS

Şanlıurfa City Guide

HISTORICAL SITES   SECTION 2

SIGNIFICANT DISTRICTS AND SITES TO VISIT

IMPORTANT PERSONAGES SECTION 4

SECTION 1
GEOGRAPHY
AND HISTORY

U rfa, situated at the cross-roads of various travel routes, has been renowned as a center of trade and culture for centuries. This is a city that acts as the connection between the eastern and western parts of Anatolia, and the roads that link the Middle East and Asia,

* Although "Şanlıurfa" is the official name of the city since 1984, "Urfa" is the historical name which is still more commonly used. Thus, throughout this book, we will refer to the city as Urfa.

as well as trade routes like the Silk Road, pass through here. This is why Urfa has always been a busy center and the cradle of a number of civilizations; it is a city that sits in the middle of a region where many cultures meet. The majority of the population to the south is Arab, to the west is Turkish, and to the east are Kurds. Urfa is situated at 30–36 degrees latitude north and 37–40 degrees longitude east, and has an altitude of 518 meters (1700 feet). The Euphrates embraces it on three sides, the north, west, and south, while to the west is the Habur, a tributary of the Euphrates. Mardin lies to the east of Urfa, with Gaziantep to the west, Adıyaman to the northwest and Diyarbakır to the north. To the south is the 223-kilometer (140 miles) long Syrian border, established by the 1921 Ankara Treaty.

Harran Ulu Cami Ruins

THE MANY NAMES OF URFA

Q *amus al-Alam* (*Kamusü'l-A'lam* – The Dictionary of the World – Şemseddin Sami, 1898) notes that in 2000 B.C., during the time of Prophet Abraham, the city was known as Ur. On Hitite tablets from the 15th century B.C. the city is referred to as the "Hur Countries." In 1000 B.C. there is reference to the city on Assyrian tablets as "Hanigalbat." In inscriptions dating to 900 B.C. Urfa is referred to as "Hatte Country." In the following centuries the region fell under Macedonian rule and was renamed "Osrhoene." In 300 B.C. the Aramaeans called the city "Urhai." The fertile area reminded the Macedonians of their homeland and they named the city after their own capital, Edessa, meaning "with abundant water." In a later period the Arabs called this city Ruha. After 640 C.E., when the region came under Muslim control, it became known as Diyar-ı Mudar. The name Urfa itself is said to be derived from the word Urhai.

THE OLDEST ARTIFACTS IN ŞANLIURFA

The oldest artifacts in Urfa were discovered on Göbekli Hill. The hill is situated in the Örencik village, twenty kilometers (twelve miles) to the east of Urfa. Here, the oldest temple mount in history was discovered. The artifacts unearthed in the excavations, which started in 1996, suggest that this mount dates back to 9000 B.C. This gives Urfa a history of 11,000 years.

The excavations carried out in Göbekli Hill, at which remnants dating back to the Neolithic period were found, revealed a sculpture workshop, the oldest in Anatolia. Here the archaeologists found sculptures of the heads of human beings, lions, boar, and bulls, as well as figurines of frogs and other animals.

The excavations also revealed religious temples, indicating that the people in this region had an organized religion. The data gleaned from here leads us to conclusions that are diametrically opposed to what had been thought earlier. The findings from around Göbekli Hill indicate that the people who were living in

9000 B.C. had a much more sophisticated lifestyle than we had hitherto imagined. According to Islamic historians, the period that Göbekli Hill belongs to corresponds to a time that is close to that in which Prophet Adam lived. The artifacts found in Göbekli Hill date civilizations in Anatolia back further than known history and change current assumptions, indicating a need for a possible revision. In addition to what has been found at Göbekli Hill, tools dating back more than 8,000 years have been found near the Birecik District of Urfa.

HISTORY OF URFA

In the light of the data revealed during the Göbekli Hill excavations, the history of Urfa can be traced

Relief of a fox on the Standing Stones at Göbekli Hill

back to 9000 B.C. or earlier. However, the information provided in this book starts from the written records, thus starting in 2500 B.C.

1. THE PERIOD OF THE EBLA AND AKKAD KINGDOMS (2500–2100 B.C.)

The Ebla Kingdom was founded in 2500 B.C. in Aleppo in North Syria. At this time, Urfa was under the rule of this kingdom. In the archaeological excavations carried out in Ebla (the capital of the kingdom) tablet inscriptions were found. These tablets have been dated to 2500 B.C., revealing that Harran, a province of Urfa, was part of this kingdom.

The Akkadian Empire (2350–2150 B.C.) is considered to be the first state in the history of Mesopotamia. The Akkadian King Sargon I (2340–2284 B.C.) conquered North Syria. Then the kingdom spread towards southeast Anatolia and Cilicia. Urfa fell within the region of North Syria at the time. The Akkadian Empire ended around 2150 B.C. with the invasion of the Gutians, who had established a state to the west of Iran.

2. THE THIRD SUMERIAN-UR DYNASTY AND ANCIENT BABYLONIA (2500 B.C.)

Some of Anatolia and Urfa came under the control of the third Sumerian-Ur dynasty (2060–1960 B.C.) during the later Akkadian period. The era of the ancient kingdom of Babylonia started when Hammurabi, the famous Babylonian king, con-

quered the region (1792–1750 B.C.). King Hammurabi seized the Mari region and the land of Assyria, Elam and its environs.

It is believed that the years from 2200 to 2000 B.C. roughly correspond to the period in which Prophet Abraham lived. Thus, we can conjecture that at that time either the Akkadian or the Sumerian-Ur dynasty was ruling the region. Although there have been suggestions that Nimrod—whom Prophet Abraham struggled against—was the Babylonian king Hammurabi (1792–1750 B.C.), the dates do not correspond.

3. THE HURRIAN-MITANNI AND HITTITE KINGDOMS (2000–1270 B.C.)

Starting from 2000 B.C. the Hurrian Kingdom existed in this region. It ruled over a very large territory, with borders expanding all the way to the Caucasus to the north, Syria and upper Mesopotamia to the south, the Toros Mountains to the west and Umriye Lake beyond the Zagros Mountains in Iran to the east. It has been established that the Hurrians spoke a language related to the languages of Central Asia.

The name Hurri, which means "cave" in Babylonian, is thought to have been given to this kingdom due to the large number of caves that are found in the Urfa region. It is also thought that the center of the Hurrian Kingdom was Urfa. In tablets inscribed in the Hittite language that

View towards the north of the city from the castle, Dergah Park

date back to 1500 B.C. Urfa is referred to as the "Hurri Countries," supporting this theory.

The Hittites, on the other hand, established their state in 1800 B.C. in Anatolia. It is known that their capital was Hattusas (Boğazköy). In 1600 B.C. they conquered Aleppo in Syria. At that time the Hurrian Kingdom reigned over southeastern Anatolia. In a conflict between the two kingdoms, the Hurrian Kingdom was defeated and retreated. When the Hittites took Aleppo, they also defeated the Mari Kingdom. Then they followed the Euphrates and came south to Babylon. They took Babylon in 1605 and ransacked it, returning home with the spoils of war. Up until 1600 B.C. Mursilish I was the king of the Hittites. After he was killed, Hantili I ascended

the throne and reigned in this region from 1600–1570 B.C.

Around 1600 B.C. the Hurris still continued to control certain parts of Anatolia, stretching their domain from the Mediterranean in the west, to the region of Kirkuk in the east. From between 1500 and 1450 B.C., however, the Hurris divided into two separate kingdoms, with one remaining the Hurrian Kingdom, while the other became known as the Mitanni State. It is known that the capital of the Mitanni Kingdom was what forms the Ceylanpınar district of Urfa today. By the end of the 1400 B.C., the influence of the Hurrian Kingdom had come to an end and the whole region fell under the control of the Mitanni Kingdom. In this period the Mitanni Kingdom consisted of the provinces of

Kargamış, Harran, Urfa, Aleppo and Antakya.

The Mitannis conquered the land of the Subarus in 1453 B.C. The Mitanni king, Shaushtatar, conquered the city of Assyria after the conquest of the Subarus. During the reign of King Shaushtatar the borders of the Mitannis expanded further and they reached the Zagros Mountains to the east. They then re-conquered the Aleppo and Kadesh districts in northern Syria, which they had lost for a while. Later the Mitanni Kingdom was constantly struggling with the Hittites.

With the rule of the Hurrian Kingdom in Anatolia, the Mitanni Kingdom started to collapse. The Hurrian Kingdom established Urfa as its capital while the Mitannis remained in control of southeastern Anatolia.

The Hittites took Aleppo and lands to the west of the Euphrates in 1377 B.C. The Hittite king Suppiluliuma I conquered Washshukanni, the capital of the Mitanni Kingdom, as well as northern Syria in 1366 B.C. and ransacked them both. One of the sons of the Hittite king killed the Mitanni king Tushratta when the Hittites entered the capital Washshukanni. At the time, the Assyrian kingdom was on the rise in the region. The Hittite king thought that the Assyrians might be a threat and started to seek solutions to this problem. He gave his daughter in marriage to Mattiwaza, the younger son of the late king, Tusratta. Mattiwaza made a pact with the Hittite king and this agreement forced the Mitanni Kingdom to be dependent on the Hittites, which eventually led to the decline of the Mitanni nation.

The Hittite king Suppiluliuma I later conquered Carchemish and Harran and expanded his territory. In 1345 B.C. Suppiluliuma died and then various states within the kingdom declared their independence, for example, Arzava, Kizzuvatna and Mitanni.

The Mitanni king Sattuara I (reign 1320–1300 B.C.) attacked the Assyrians, seeing that they were growing in power. However, the Assyrian king Adad-Nirari I (1307–1274 B.C.) defeated the Mitannis. Later, the Assyrian king Adad-Nirari I tried to take control of Hanigalbat, which was under Mitanni rule. The Mitanni king of the time, Wasashatta (1300–1280 B.C.), made war preparations with a large army at a place called Irridu, somewhere between Carchemish and Harran. The Mitanni king Wasashatta was taken captive during the war with the Assyrians in 1275 B.C., and this spelt the end of the Mitanni kingdom. By the time the Hittite kingdom collapsed in 1200 B.C., the Assyrians had greatly expanded their control over Anatolia.

It is believed that what remains of the Mitanni civilization today are the conical houses in Harran. Another piece of information about the Mitannis that has reached us is that they were very good at breeding horses.

4. THE ARAMAEANS AND THE ASSYRIAN KINGDOM (1270–610 B.C.)

In 1000 B.C. the Assyrians and Aramaeans, Semitic peoples, ruled Anatolia. In this period the Aramaeans moved from the south of Anatolia to the southeast. For a long period many Aramaean groups migrated and settled in upper Mesopotamia, establishing a state there. One of these states was known as Bit-Adini (Beth Eden), and was centered in the Urfa region. The Assyrians struggled against the reign of the Aramaeans in Anatolia, and in 875–866 B.C. the Assyrians managed to put an end to the reign of the Bit-Adini, seizing Urfa.

Another state that reigned in Anatolia at that time was the Urartu Kingdom, which ruled the regions around Lake Van. The borders of the Urartu Kingdom were established in 900 B.C., and stretched to the Caucasus in the north, Iran in the east, Malatya in the northwest and Urfa-Halfeti in the south. For 300 years the Urartu Kingdom fought against the Assyrians. In 743 B.C. the Assyrian king Tiglath-Pileser III (745–727 B.C.) fought with the Urartu army in the north of the Halfeti district of Urfa, and defeated them. After this war, northern Syria and Urfa once again fell under the rule of the Assyrians.

THE CHALDEAN (NEW BABYLON) AND MEDO-PERSIAN KINGDOMS (610–330 B.C.)

The long-standing sovereignty of the Assyrian Kingdom in Anatolia was weakened by the death of King Ashurbanipal in 626 B.C. and shortly afterwards the kingdom disintegrated. After the death of the king, the separate kingdoms of the Medo-Persians and the Chaldeans started to rule over the region.

In the final stages of the Assyrian Kingdom, the Mede King Cyaxares (635–584 B.C.) joined forces with the Babylonian Nabopolassar and in 614. B.C. they seized the former capital of Calah and Nineveh. They killed the Assyrian king Sinsharishkun (623–612 B.C) in battle. After this, the Assyrian Kingdom was divided between the Meds and the Chaldeans. The surviving members of the Assyrian army came to Harran, establishing this city as the capital of Assyria. The state that was established with this final effort did not last long; two years later the Babylonians seized it and the Assyrian state was thus totally eliminated. The famous Temple of Sin that had been in Harran for many years was destroyed during these wars.

In this period the Lydian Kingdom was extremely powerful in western Anatolia. In eastern Anatolia the Med Kingdom grew and started to represent a threat to the Lydian Kingdom. When these two kingdoms made a peace agreement, the Mede king Cyaxares diverted his attention completely to the east and continued his conquests. The Meds also defeated the Urartus, who were in a weak posi-

tion then. At the same time, the Chaldeans, who ruled over Harran, joined forces with the Persians to declare war on the Meds.

The last Chaldean king Nabonidus (Nabu-na'id) (556–538 B.C.) and the Persian king Cyrus (reign 559–530 B.C.) acted in unison and defeated the Meds in three years. In 550 B.C. the Chaldean king Nabuna'id restored the Temple of Sin in Harran, which had been destroyed. This temple continued to stand until the conquest of Harran by Islamic armies in 640 C.E. In 539 B.C. the Chaldean (New Babylon) Kingdom was destroyed by the Persian king Cyrus. After that date, Urfa and Harran were ruled by the Persians.

Urfa and Harran were part of the Babylon and Syria Satrapy; the Aramaic language and script used in Urfa and Harran during that period were adopted as the official language and script of the Persian Empire and were used throughout the whole of Anatolia. Later, during the reign of Darius I (reign 522–486 B.C.) the Urfa and Harran region became part of the Babylon Satrapy. In this period the Persians were cultivating the land between the Euphrates and Tigris Rivers and they made great developments in agriculture.

THE MACEDONIAN and SELEUCID KINGDOMS (330–132 B.C.)

In the 330 B.C. the Macedonian Kingdom was the rising force in

Göbekli Hill - Standing Stones

Anatolia. The Macedonians entered Anatolia in 334 B.C. under the leadership of Alexander the Great and defeated the Persian armies. Later, Alexander defeated the Persian armies again in 332 B.C. in Issos (Dörtyol), near Hatay. This hailed the beginning of Macedonian rule in Urfa and southeast Anatolia. The Urfa region was called Osrhoene and Harran was known as Mygdonia during Macedonian rule. During this period many Macedonian and Greek people settled here, thus transferring Greek culture to the area. Today we know that the religious life here was affected by the Greek religion and that the gods were given Greek names.

After the settlement of eastern Anatolia by the Macedonians, there was an interaction between Greek and eastern cultures. Hellenic culture started to dominate the area. In the first centuries after Christ we see that Christian culture dominated the region. The Edessa Kingdom in Urfa adopted Christianity in the very early stages, thus making Urfa a very important Christian center.

Harran also continued to be a great center for Hellenic culture, and idol worship was prevalent here. Thus, Harran was known as Hellenopolis for a long time. With the dominance of Hellenic culture in southeast Anatolia, this culture was carried over to the Arabs via the Aramaeans. The spread of Hellenic culture in Anatolia and among the Arabs was largely facilitated by the wide use of the Aramaic language.

When the Macedonian king Alexander died in 323 B.C. there was a power struggle among his commanders, and a war began, with a great scramble for the empire. After these wars, the southeastern Anatolia region was divided up. In 306 B.C. the general that ruled Babylonia, Seleucus Nicator, declared himself to be king of the region. King Seleucus Nicator ruled over a wide region, including Harran. King Seleucus Nicator now ruled over lands that had formerly belonged to the Persian Empire and he established the city of Seleucia on the banks of the Tigris; this empire became known as the Seleucid Empire.

In 302 B.C. King Seleucus Nicator I established the city of Urfa on the ruins of an earlier settlement. He named this new city Edessa. This was also the name of the capital city of Macedonia at the time, and meant "place of abundant water." At the time Urfa was also a green city with a great deal of water resources; in this period the Aramaeans called the city Urhai. The important cities in Mesopotamia at the time were Edessa, Carrhae (Harran), Makedonopolis (Birecik), Nikephorion (Rakka) and Anthemusia (Suruç).

The Egyptian pharaoh Ptolemy Evergetes led campaigns into southeastern Anatolia around 240 B.C. The pharaoh defeated the army of the Seleucids, crossed the Euphrates and advanced towards the north. He then seized the region of Urfa from the Seleucids in 245 B.C. Shortly afterwards, the Seleucid king Kallinikos joined forces with the Pontus state to the north and recaptured Antioch and Urfa. In 140 B.C. a war took place between the Parthians and Seleucids around the Zagros Mountains. In this war the Parthians took Iran and Mesopotamia from the Seleucids. What can be gathered from the available historical documents is that Balıklı Göl (Fish Lake) existed in Urfa at this period and was called "the Seleucid Lake" or "Seleucos Lake."

5. THE OSRHOENE (EDESSA) KINGDOM (132 B.C. – 244 C.E.)

The Seleucids had been weakened by the war with the Parthians. As a result, the Assyrians established their own kingdom in 132 B.C., the Osrhoene Kingdom, with Edessa as

Roman ruins in Eski Hisar, Büyük Keşişlik (Great Monastery) Village

the capital. The kingdom was established under the leadership of Aryu. This was the first kingdom in the Urfa region.

During this period the Parthians reigned over Syria. In 53 B.C. the Romans came to Syria to fight the Parthians; after taking a few cities the Romans crossed the Euphrates and reached Harran via Rakka. The Roman army, led by General Crassus, was defeated in Harran in the battle against the Parthians and General Crassus was taken captive. Some of the Roman army managed to flee after the war.

The Edessa Kingdom that was set up in Urfa encountered Christianity during the reign of King Abgar V (13–50 C.E.). Before Christianity, the Mesopotamian region followed pagan traditions; it was common to find the moon, the sun, the stars and the planets being worshipped as gods.

In the region of Urfa, and particularly in Harran, "Sin, the Moon God" had a large impact on the regional culture, with there being many great temples dedicated to this god. Writings and motifs pertaining to the belief system of the period can still be seen in the ruins around the Soğmatar district of Harran. During the reign of the Edessa king, Abgar V, the people of Urfa converted to Christianity and great changes took place in the spiritual life of the region. The Edessa Kingdom in Urfa was the first state in history to accept Christianity.

According to legend, King Abgar V suffered from leprosy. Although the king had heard that Jesus cured lepers, he was so badly afflicted by the disease that he could not go to Jerusalem to be cured. He sent an envoy called Hannan to Jesus with a letter declaring that he had accepted Christianity, asking about Jesus' teachings and inviting him to Urfa.

The envoy Hannan was also a very good artist. After presenting the letter to Jesus he climbed on a high platform and tried to paint Jesus' portrait, but could not manage to do so. Understanding that the artist had been unable to depict him, Jesus washed his face and then dried it on a handkerchief, giving it to Hannan. Those around him could see that Jesus' portrait had been imprinted on this piece of cloth. Hannan took a letter and this cloth back to Edessa. Jesus sent the apostle Thomas in his place and he prayed for the king. King Abgar put this cloth on his wounds and was miraculously cured of his leprosy.

This cloth was kept for many centuries; however, its location is no longer known. According to certain oral traditions, it fell into the well in the Great Mosque in Urfa, and thus the well is considered to be sacred. It is also said that the contents of the letter Jesus sent to King Abgar were inscribed over the entrance of a cave in Urfa, but it is not known where the original letter is. No trace remains of the letter or the cave. The legend of this sacred handkerchief has remained in Christian folklore and art for many centuries.

In the first century C.E. the Roman Empire's influence could be felt throughout the Urfa region. The Roman emperor Trajanus came to Urfa in 114, and he was warmly welcomed by the king of Edessa, Abgar VII (reign 109–116).

Then around 116 a general rebellion against Roman occupation broke out in Mesopotamia, and Urfa joined this movement. At first the Roman forces were defeated, but then later they mounted a revenge attack on Urfa, killing many people and burning the city down.

After this war King Abgar VII's reign came to an end and Urfa was now in the hands of the Romans. However, this rule continued for only one year, with the region being taken by the Parthians.

In the following years the Roman influence became stronger. In 163 there was a disagreement between the two great powers, the Parthians and

Üçayak Mosaic

Büyük Keşişlik Village Roman Ruins

the Romans. The Romans defeated the Parthians and took most of Mesopotamia. The Roman General Avidius Cassius laid siege to Urfa, where the citizens slaughtered the Parthian Garrison and let in the Romans. After that, Urfa and Harran once again fell under Roman rule. This continued until the collapse of Western Rome in 244.

The Romans set up stations all over the region both to consolidate their rule and to control attacks by the Iranians. In 197 Emperor Septimius Severus I had castles built to protect his land, particularly from the Parthians, between Halfeti and Urfa, and in the villages of Eski Hisar, Büyük Keşişlik, and Ank. They also built watchtowers in different parts of the region. One can still see these ruins, which can be found within the triangle that lies between Halfeti, Suruç and Urfa.

During this period great rivers flowed through Urfa. Floods were caused by these rivers, with the first that we know of happening in 201. In this catastrophe more than 2,000 people were drowned or killed under structures that collapsed. Some important landmarks were also destroyed in this flood, including the royal palace.

After the destruction of the palace, the king, Abgar the Great (VIII), had a great palace built within the fortress walls. In 213 the Osrhoene province in Urfa was invaded once again by the Roman emperor Antoninus Caracalla.

The king of Urfa, Abgar Severus X, and his sons were taken prisoner and brought to Rome, where they were executed. Urfa once again had come under Roman rule. The Roman emperor Antoninus Caracalla was murdered by his own soldiers in 217, somewhere between Urfa and Harran.

Between 214 and 240 Manu IX was King of Urfa; however, his presence was hardly felt, as the region was under Roman control. The name Manu is inscribed on one of the two pillars, known as the catapult at the fort in Urfa; this Manu may well have been the same king. In the period between 242 and 244, when Abgar Phrahates IX was king in Urfa, the Roman Emperor Philippus Arabs made an agreement with the Sassanid king Shahpur I, and gave Mesopotamia over to the Sassanids. Later this agreement was broken and as a result the Osrhoene Kingdom disappeared completely. Harran once again fell under Roman control.

Different beliefs abounded in Urfa region in 376, a time when Urfa was still part of the Assyrian Kingdom. This was also a very rich environment for languages, art and literature. It was in this period that the Bible was translated for the first time from the Greek into the Assyrian language; this took place in Urfa. Edessa culture, which was very strong in the Urfa region, was a fusion of Greek, Persian and Aramaean-Assyrian cultures. One can see the influence of the Greco-Roman style in the cultural and architectural works of the region. Many of these works can still be seen in the city of Urfa itself and in the museum; here there are good examples of mosaics, inscriptions and different stelae.

6. THE ROMAN EMPIRE (244–395)

During the time the Roman Empire ruled over Urfa and its environs the Christian people and clergymen suffered great oppression from the Romans. In 250 some of the Christian population and priests were killed. Sharbil and Barsamya were among the priests who were killed, and their graves are located in what is today the Şehitlik district of Urfa. Where they were buried a small church was built in their memory.

During this period, the Sassanid Kingdom gained power in Mesopotamia and Eastern Anatolia. In 253 the Sassanid King Shahpur I started to rule over Armenia and advanced towards Mesopotamia. The Sassanids gathered forces to attack Urfa; however, they had a hard time conquering the city. The Roman emperor Valerianus decided to stop the Sassanids. In a war that took place in 260 Emperor Valerianus fell captive to the Sassanids and was killed. However, the Sassanids did not manage to take Urfa. In 359 Edessa became the capital of the Osrhoene province, which had been re-established in 359 by the Roman emperor Constantine.

In 373 the Assyrian Orthodox Christians in Urfa were harassed by the Romans once again, with most of them being expelled from the city. In 395 the Roman Empire was divided into the Eastern and Western Roman Empire. The Oshroene district, in which Urfa is situated, became part of the Eastern Roman (Byzantine) Empire.

In the Roman period one of the most important cities in the Urfa region was Zeugma. The Fourth Scythian Legion was stationed in this strategic town. Today, Zeugma lies buried under the Birecik dam. Conservation excavations were carried out here, which is also called the "Belkıs ruins," by the Gaziantep Museum and some of the artifacts that were discovered are now on display.

7. THE BYZANTINE EMPIRE AND THE SASSANID EMPIRE (395–639)

The year 395 marked the beginning of Eastern Roman rule, or the Byzantine period, in Urfa. In 500 a swarm of locusts destroyed all the crops in the city and caused a great famine; as a result, some of the population died of hunger, while others moved to other cities. A year later a very harsh winter hit Urfa, again causing many deaths. Some reports say that the number of dead was as many as 2,000. In this period, the powerful Sassanid Kingdom tried to capture Urfa and its environs. In 502 the Sassanid king Kubad I (488–531) first moved to take Diyarbakır and then sent his troops to Harran and Viranşehir. The same year the Sassanids laid siege to Urfa, but were impeded by the strong ramparts around the city. In the following years King Kubad I returned without having established peace.

Halepli Garden, Amazon Queen
Mosaic detail

After having undergone three great floods in earlier years, Urfa then suffered a fourth flood, in which it is said that 30,000 people died. This number corresponds to half the population of the city. After this catastrophe the Roman emperor Justinian had a dam built and changed the course of the Daysan River to prevent future floods. The remains of these walls can still be seen today.

There were many battles between the two great powers of the period: the Sassanid and the Byzantine Empires. In 532 the two sides signed a peace treaty. The agreement lasted eight years and then the Sassanids broke the peace. The Sassanid king at the time, Khosrau I, occupied Aleppo, Alexandretta and Humus in 540 and laid siege to Urfa, but failed to conquer the city. Later in 544 he attempted once again to take Urfa, however he failed yet again. The Sassanids organized many campaigns against Byzantine lands and pillaged the region. However, in 581 the Byzantine commander Maurikios (Maurice) managed to defeat the Sassanid army in the region of Viranşehir and Rakka.

The Sassanids, who had been trying for a very long time to seize Urfa, managed to do so in 610. Thus, with the conquest of Urfa by Khosrau II, the Byzantine influence in the region was partially eliminated. During this period the Sassanids severely persecuted the Christians in the region and ransacked the churches. The Sassanid rule did not last long and in 628 the

The Wall that Changed the Course of the Daysan River

Byzantine emperor Heraclius took Urfa, restoring Byzantine rule.

8. THE FOUR CALIPHS (639–661)

The Byzantine Empire ruled for about 230 years in Urfa. In 639, during the rule of the Caliph Umar, the commander of the Damascene forces, Iyadh ibn Ghanam, captured Urfa and the city was subjected to taxation. Upper Mesopotamia was divided into three after the Islamic conquest; the three regions were known as Diyar al-Mudar, Diyar al-Rabia and Diyar al-Bakr. The center of Diyar al-Mudar was Harran, with the other major cities being Urfa, Rakka and Suruç.

Urfa fell under the reign of Muawiyah, the governor of Damascus, during the rule of Caliph Uthman. When Caliph Ali was assassinated in 661, the Umayyad State was established under the leadership of Muawiyah, with Urfa as part of this state.

9. THE UMAYYADS (661–750)

Urfa and Harran remained under Umayyad rule between 661 and 750. When Marwan II (744–750) became caliph in 744 he transferred the center of the caliphate to Harran. Much investment was put into the ancient city after it had become the seat of the caliphate.

Caliph Marwan II spent ten million dirhams on these new investments. He first had a Government Palace built and then he renovated the Ulu Cami (Grand Mosque). One can still visit the ruins of this mosque today. Then Marwan II had irrigation canals built for farming and to encourage commerce. The region of Urfa-Harran, which was also known as al-Jazira, enjoyed its heyday during the era of Marwan. As a result of investments, the tax revenues from the region also increased substantially.

The Umayyad rule continued until 750, when the Abbasids became the dominant power. First, the Abbasids took over much of Iran and Mesopotamia. After this, Marwan II prepared an army and engaged in a great battle with the Abbasids along the Zap River in 750. Marwan II was defeated and the whole of al-Jazira fell into the hands of the Abbasids.

One of the most important events in the region during the Umayyad period was the great flood of Urfa that occurred in 667. This flooding was the fifth recorded flood in Urfa. The city walls around Urfa were destroyed and many thousands were drowned. Another important event happened in 679, when an earthquake caused the death of many inhabitants.

10. THE ABBASIDS (750– 990)

After the Umayyads, the Abbasid commander Abdullah ibn Ali took control over the region in 750 and appointed Musa ibn Ka'b as governor of al-Jazira. Having gained control over the region, the Abbasids persecuted the Umayyads. The Arabs of Syria and al-Jazira rebelled in the face of this oppression. The commander who took these lands, Abdullah ibn Ali, violently suppressed the rebellion. Many years later rebellions broke out in the region again. A rebellion in 812, led by two men called Amr and Nasr ibn Shabas, resulted in the pillage of Urfa, Harran and Suruç. Baghdad, which was the seat of the caliphate during the Abbasid period, had difficulty suppressing the rebellion, which continued for thirteen years. Finally it was quashed in 825, and the perpetrators were hanged.

After another long period, the Byzantine armies approached Urfa once again in 943. The Byzantine commander, General Ioannes Kurkuas, wanted to take the cloth that was believed to have the imprint of Jesus' face. The Muslims signed a treaty with the Byzantines and in return for the release of 200 Muslim prisoners, the sacred cloth was presented to the Byzantines. The cloth was then taken to the capital of the Byzantine Empire – Constantinople.

In 949 the people of Urfa joined forces with the Hamdanis and attacked the Byzantine lands. Thus, the treaty was annulled, and in 959 the Byzantines sent an army to al-Jazira and Urfa under the command of Leon. In this war many civilians were killed and some were taken prisoner.

Mukimu Mosaic

Another important event in this period was the great flood of 835, the seventh of its kind in Urfa, which killed 3,000 people.

11. THE HAMDANIS, NUMAYRIS AND MARWANIS (991–1031)

The rule of the Mosul Hamdanis, who controlled Harran, ended in 937. Later Sa'duddawla, who reigned in Aleppo, took Harran. Upon the death of Sa'duddawla in 991, the principalities under his dominion declared their independence. Wassab Sabiq al-Numayri, the governor of Harran at the time, declared his independence as well. In this period Urfa fell under the control of the Numayri dynasty. The Marwani ruler Nasruddawla Ahmed, who ruled in

Diyarbakır, sent an army to take Urfa. In the war that was fought in 1027 against the Numayris, Urfa fell completely into the hands of Nasruddawla Ahmed; he then appointed the commander Salman to govern the city. In 1031 the Byzantine commander Georgios Maniakes captured the city.

12. THE BYZANTINE EMPIRE (1031–1087)

The years 1031–1087, during which the Byzantine Empire reigned in the Urfa region, witnessed the rise of the Great Seljuks in Anatolia. The Seljuks made many attempts to take Urfa. In 1065–1066 Salar of Khorasan carried out raids into the region of Urfa. Then the Seljuks launched a second attack and fought the Byzantines near Kısas. In this battle the Seljuk army suffered great losses and had to retreat. The Seljuks gained victory with their third attempt. The Battle of Malazgirt (Manzikert) was decisive between the Byzantines and the Great Seljuks. On his way to Egypt, Sultan Alparslan (1063–1072) first conquered some castles around Urfa. Then in 1071 he laid siege to Urfa, but he had to lift the siege after it continued for a protracted period. The Sultan was planning to go to Syria immediately after the siege, but he learned that the Byzantine army was marching eastward. Upon learning this, Alparslan immediately reversed his course back to Anatolia to confront the Byzantine army. In 1071 the Seljuks defeated the Byzantines and

Emperor Romanus IV Diogenes was taken prisoner.

After the Battle of Malazgirt Byzantine power in Anatolia weakened. After Sultan Alparslan, his son Melikşah (1054–1092) came to Harran in 1087 and sent one of his commanders, Emir Bozan, to Urfa. The siege here lasted for three months and Emir Bozan took the city within the year. After five years, Harran was turned over to Emir Bozan in 1093 without fighting.

13. THE GREAT SELJUKS AND THE SYRIAN-PALESTINIAN SELJUKS (1087–1095)

After Urfa came under Seljuk rule in 1087, the chaos and confusion in the area ended. The commander Emir Bozan left the administration of the city to the commander Salar Huluk and then joined the army of Sultan Melikşah. When Sultan Melikşah was murdered on 19 November 1092, Emir Bozan returned to Urfa. After the death of Sultan Melikşah there was a struggle for leadership in the Great Seljuk State between the son of Berkyaruk and the Syria-Palestine Seljuk sultan, Malik Tutush. Malik Tutush won the war in 1094 and had Emir Bozan and the Aleppo emir Aksungur, who supported Berkyaruk, killed. Malik Tutush sent troops to take Urfa and Harran, which were under the control of Emir Bozan. Emir Bozan's soldiers, who were in the city at the time, did not want to hand over the city at first, but in the end they did. Malik Tutush thus took over Urfa and

then handed its administration over to Thoros, who was of Armenian descent. With the death of Malik Tutush in 1095, Thoros declared his rule over Urfa.

14. ARMENIAN THOROS (1095–1098) AND THE CRUSADER EARLDOM (1098–1144)

The reign of Armenian Thoros lasted only three years. In 1097 a great crusader army came to Anatolia and reached Antioch. Here, the commander's younger brother, Baldwin, separated from the main army with a group of 700 soldiers and moved towards the Euphrates River. Baldwin seized a number of fortresses and towns to the west of the river. Upon an invitation from Thoros, he came to Urfa with 200 knights. However, soon afterwards, in 1098, Thoros was killed during an insurrection and the next day Baldwin became the count of Urfa.

When his brother, who had set up his own earldom in Jerusalem, died, Baldwin was invited to Jerusalem. Baldwin appointed his cousin Baldwin du Bourcq to rule Urfa and he left the city in 1100, after forcefully taking a great deal of gold and silver from the people.

In 1104 the Artuk ruler Sökmen joined forces with Balduk and Çökürmüş to attack the Frankish army to take Harran. This new triple force defeated the Franks, and Baldwin II was taken prisoner. Then Çökürmüş, the ruler of Mosul, established control over Harran. After that he marched upon Urfa as well. The fifteen-day siege was inconclusive and Çökürmüş had to return to Mosul.

When the new Urfa count Baldwin du Bourcq was taken captive by Çökürmüş the Antioch count Bohemund became the ruler of Urfa. He ruled Urfa until 1108. During this period the Anatolian Seljuk sultan Kılıçarslan I (1092–1107) tried to take Urfa. He advanced until he reached the outskirts of the city, but failed to conquer it. However, he turned south and took Harran.

The Crusader earldom lasted about fifty years in Urfa. In this period of oppression and atrocities, the Crusaders ravaged the Muslim territory. This period ended with Imadeddin Zengi, the ruler of Mosul, who took Urfa from the Crusaders in December 1144.

15. THE MOSUL PRINCIPALITY (ZENGIDS) (1144–1182)

After the Mosul Prince Imadeddin Zengi took Urfa in 1145 one of his first actions was to forge friendly relations with the Muslim and Christian religious leaders in the town. However, Zengi's rule did not last long and he was killed in 1146 at the Castle of Jabar. After his death, the country was divided into two; his son Seyfeddin Gazi ruled Mosul and Nureddin Mahmud ruled Aleppo. Count Jocelyn II took advantage of the weakened authority in the Urfa region, capturing the city in 1146 with the help of the Armenians. Then Nureddin Mahmud Zengi immediately prepared an army and came to Urfa. In the war that ensued, tens of thousands of people died. Jocelyn II could not withstand Nureddin Mahmud's army and fled Urfa. With the recapture of the city by the Turks, the preparations for the second Crusade began in Europe.

With the death of Nureddin Mahmud Zengi on 15 May 1174, unrest started once again, but this situation did not continue for long. Seyfeddin Gazi II, the nephew of the deceased sultan, mobilized his armies, taking Harran, Urfa, Rakka and Suruç under his control.

During this period Saladin (Salahaddin Ayyubi) ruled Egypt. Saladin had been one of Nureddin Mahmud Zengi's commanders and after Nureddin's death in 1174 he established the state of the Ayyubids in Egypt. Then he directed his attention to the region of Urfa. At this time, Harran was ruled by Muzaffereddin Gökbörü, who was loyal to the Zengids. Gökbörü sent word to Saladin declaring his allegiance.

Upon being informed of this, Saladin organized a campaign to the region, coming all the way to Birecik Castle. Here Muzaffereddin Gökbörü joined forces with him. The commander ruling Birecik Castle also declared allegiance to Saladin. After tak-

Two pillars in the Urfa Castles, believed to be part of the catapult with which Abraham was cast into the fire

ing Birecik, Saladin moved towards Urfa. During the great siege of Urfa in September 1182, the governor of the town, Fahreddin Mesud Zaferani, fought against Saladin, but could not hold the town for long. Finally, he handed the city over to Saladin and entered his service. Saladin appointed Fahreddin Mesud Zaferani as governor of Urfa and Harran.

16. THE EGYPTIAN AND SYRIAN AYYUBIDS (1182–1260)

The Ayyubid presence in Anatolia led to a power struggle with the Anatolian Seljuks. After Saladin, al-Kamil Nasreddin I (1218–1238) became the head of the Ayyubid state in Egypt. In 1232 al-Kamil Nasreddin I ruled over a vast region, including Urfa, Harran and Siverek. At this time Sultan Alaeddin Keykubad I ruled the Anatolian Seljuk State. When Alaeddin Keykubad I was in the city of Malatya with his army, he sent his commander Kemaleddin Kamyar to Urfa. In 1235 the Seljuks laid siege to Urfa and met great resistance, but in the end they managed to conquer the castle. The Seljuk army then went on to take the region of Siverek, Harran and Rakka. This Seljuk control over the region did not last long. After four months the Ayyubid sultan al-Kamil Nasreddin I regained all the territory that had been lost to the Seljuks. After two years the Khwarazmians, who had been loyal to the Seljuks, broke away and moved towards the region of Urfa. In 1240, the Seljuks sent an army against the Khwarazmians and defeated them in Harran, leaving Harran to the Ayyubids.

In this period the Mongols advanced into Anatolia and caused havoc in the region. The Mongol khan Hulagu launched two campaigns on Urfa. In the first one in 1251 he entered Urfa, Suruç and Harran and ransacked them. In the second campaign, at the start of 1260, Hulagu Khan conquered Harran, Urfa and Birecik while on his way to Syria.

17. THE MAMLUKS AND TURKMEN TRIBES (1260–1394)

The Mongol influence in Urfa lasted until 1272. At the time, Baybars I appointed Alaeddin Taybars as governor of Aleppo. In 1272 Alaeddin Taybars took Harran and Urfa from the Mongols. Two years later he also took Birecik and made this region a part of the Mamluk Empire.

In 1318 a period of decline and division began for the Anatolian Seljuk State. The different Turkmen tribes started to gain power. Among them, the Döğer tribe of the Oghuz Turkmen settled in Urfa. In a short time they took Urfa, Siverek, Suruç and Harran under their control.

18. THE TIMURIDS, AKKOYUNLUS, KARAKOYUNLUS, THE DULKADIR PRINCIPALITY, AND THE SAFAVIDS (1394–1517)

Jug from Timur Period (TUEM)

The reign of the Turkmen tribes in the Urfa region continued until 1394. Then Timur came and conquered Urfa, causing much destruction. The Mamluks attacked Urfa in 1429, sacking the city. After the Mamluks, Urfa came under Karakoyunlu rule. The Akkoyunlu ruler Uzun Hasan Bey (1453–1478) defeated the Karakoyunlus in Urfa in 1453 and took the town. In 1504, the city came under the rule of the Dulkadiroğulları principality.

During this period, the Iranian Safavid Empire increased its influence in Anatolia. Shah Ismail gained control over almost the whole of eastern Anatolia except for Diyarbakır. The Akkoyunlu State, situated in eastern Anatolia at the time, could not defend itself against the Safavids. The Akkoyunlu ruler Sultan Murad sought refuge with the Ottomans against the Safavids. In 1514 he received military support from Sultan Selim I, and he declared war on the Safavids; however, he was defeated and killed. In 1514 the Safavids took control of Urfa, but this reign lasted only three years.

19. THE OTTOMAN PERIOD (1517–1922)

In the east of Anatolia the Safavid State had started to present a threat to the Ottoman State. Sultan Selim I led a campaign into the region in 1517 and took Urfa and Mardin. Urfa, with a population of 5,500, became part of the Diyarbakır Principality during the Ottoman period. In 1594 the Ottomans established the Rakka Province in this region, making Urfa the capital.

Karayazıcı Abdulhalim rebelled

against the Ottoman state in 1599. He conquered Urfa and declared independence. The Ottoman state sent an army to quash the rebellion, which was led by Sinan Paşazade Mehmed Pasha; they laid siege to Urfa twice. The first siege was not successful, but in the second siege, in the spring of 1600, Urfa was recaptured.

In 1638 the Ottoman sultan Murad IV (1623–1640) went on campaign to Baghdad. En route, he visited Urfa, Harran and Viranşehir, staying a while and visiting religious sites. He initiated the search for the graves of Prophets Job and Elisha and had shrines built for them.

In 1839 the governor of Egypt, Mehmed Ali Pasha of Kavala, rebelled against the weakened central Ottoman authority and declared his sovereignty. The sultan at the time, Mahmud II, sent an army to suppress the rebellion. The army, led by Hafız Mehmet Pasha, went into battle against the army of Ibrahim Pasha, the son of Mehmed Ali Pasha, in Birecik in 1839. The Ottoman army was defeated and Ibrahim Pasha's men marched upon Urfa and occupied the city. For four years the city remained under Egyptian rule. After four years the Ottomans recaptured the region. No serious events occurred in Urfa from this time until the beginning of the twentieth century.

Urfa has been under the rule of many states, and various civilizations have passed through it. Being on the Silk Road, it was pillaged by many armies and suffered many atrocities. During the Ottoman period the city enjoyed a time of peace and tranquility. However, after 500 years of peace, the city once again underwent a great ordeal in the 20th century.

During the final years of the Ottoman Empire, at the start of the 1900's, the Armenians living in Urfa rebelled many times. The Armenians, who had lived in peace with the Muslims in Urfa for centuries, rebelled due to the weakened condition of the Ottoman Empire and foreign instigation. Foreign powers also provided arms for the insurgent groups. The first rebellion occurred in 1915. The rebellion was quashed by a military police force of between twenty and thirty men, with one of the officers dying during the conflict. After this, a search was initiated and the security forces found 820 rifles, 406 pistols, 74 assault weapons and 4,922 cartridges. In 1925 the attacks by the insurgent Armenian groups continued and many people died—not only military personnel, but civilians as well.

At this time the state was unable to protect its citizens against insurgent groups. The help of the Fourth Army Corps was called for. The general, Ahmed Cemal Pasha, came to Urfa, but the rebellion continued. The rebels killed many innocent people, including women and children. On 16 October 1915 the strongholds of the Armenian rebels were destroyed and the rebellion ended. There had

Balıklıgöl (Fish Lake) and Rıdvaniye Mosque

*Güllüzade Hacı Osman Efendi, Member of
Urfa Defense of Rights Organization*

20. THE WAR OF INDEPENDENCE

In 1919 Anatolia was occupied from all directions. Southeast Anatolia was divided up by the British and the French, with Urfa being occupied on 24 March 1919 by the British. A number of British officers first came to Urfa in an armored car. They then entered Urfa with 200 soldiers, 10 jeeps and 50 trucks.

Immediately upon arriving in Urfa, the British told the Turkish soldiers to leave the city. The commander of the First Cavalry, Major Hüseyin Bey, left a cavalry troop in Urfa under the command of an officer and took his squadron to Karaköprü and then to Siverek.

The British were helped by the Armenians during their stay in Urfa. The British trained the Armenians in the use of weapons and the Armenians helped them by providing local intelligence.

been many losses during these insurgencies. Twenty soldiers and police officers had been killed and fifty injured. There were forty-two civilian casualties and many more had been injured. The number of Armenian insurgents killed was 349. As a result of this event some of the Armenians in Urfa were sent to Mosul.

Similar Armenian insurgencies occurred in other parts of eastern Anatolia as well and these reached great proportions in other towns. Because of these clashes many people migrated to Urfa from Van, Muş and Bitlis in 1916. With the increasing population, cultivatable land decreased and this led to a great famine in 1917. Many people died during the famine and illness spread during this period.

The elders of Urfa decided that something should be done about this occupation, and they gathered at the house of Güllüzade Hacı Osman Efendi on the night of 4 September 1919; here important decisions were made. The twelve people who met here established the Defense of Rights Organization, and they swore to fight until Urfa was free again.

In October 1919 the British and the French signed an agreement, and the British handed Urfa over to the French. During this time, Major Ali

A Group of French Occupation Soldiers in Urfa (Archive of Müslim Akalın, Att.)

Rıza Bey of Urfa tried to include the local clans within the framework of the Defense of Rights Organization. The head of the Siyala clan, Salih el-Abdullah, however, reported this to the French, and Ali Rıza Bey was removed from his post. After this incident the French soldiers started treating the population more harshly.

Lieutenant Ali Saip Bey was appointed to Major Ali Rıza Bey's position as head of the Urfa Gendarmerie. When he came to Urfa he also expressed ideas about a rebellion to the elders of Urfa. The idea was agreed upon, and plans were made. After this meeting, the French command invited Ali Saip Bey to tea, and it was during the tea party that he understood the French had learned about their plans for resistance. Ali Saip Bey left Urfa the same night with a group of compatriots.

The event that ignited the independence movement in Urfa occurred on 24 January 1920, when two French soldiers forced their way into the women's section of the Vezir baths. This led to an outcry in the city. Immediately after this event protests began, including those lodged by Ali Rıza Bey.

One day after the event at the baths Mustafa Kemal sent a directive to the army. In this it was stated that the action of the Kuvay-ı Milliye (National Forces) against the French should not be delayed and that it should start in Urfa.

The first action in Urfa began with Ali Saip Bey's declaration in Suruç. Here, the clans destroyed some sections of the railway and sent a missive to the French warning them to leave the town. Ali Saip Bey advanced towards Urfa with forces he had collected from among the clans. Then he re-

peated his demand that the occupying French forces leave Urfa in 24 hours. The French commander received the message, but replied that such a decision could only be made by General Gouraud. Ali Saip Bey entered Urfa on 9 February and surrounded the French forces. On 17 February, Reserve Officer Akif (Sözeri) and his men attacked the French and seized Külaflı Hill; as a result, the enemy forces had to retreat. After that, on 20 February there was another raid on the French and on the communication station that the Armenians and French used.

In March 1920 the tribal forces carried out a general attack on the French. Eighty-two people from the Urfa ranks died in this attack, and it also took its toll on the Urfa forces and tribal leaders. The Defense of Rights Organization wrote to Mustafa Kemal, asking for weapons and other military equipment. Mustafa Kemal sent a telegraph to the Thirteenth Army and Fifth Division Commandership, saying that the enemy was only located in a few buildings in Urfa and that there was no cause for alarm. In this telegraph he also stated that the affairs in Urfa were run by men who had no experience in warfare and that a commander from the army should be sent.

Under siege, the French ran out of provisions. They requested aid from the French government, but when no help came, they began to think of evacuating Urfa.

War Veterans at 11 April Independence Celebrations in Urfa (Archive of Müslim Akalın, Att.)

The French, who now understood that they were not going to win in Urfa, declared that they would leave the city. Governor Ali Rıza Bey, Ali Saip Bey, Mayor Hacı Mustafa, the French commander Hauger, Lieutenant Sajous and the Armenian doctor Beşliyan, all gathered at a meeting on 9 April 1920 and came to an agreement as to how to end the occupation in Urfa. The French stipulated ten conditions before they would leave the town; these were all accepted. The most important of these conditions were the guarantee of the safety of the Armenians who were living in Urfa, the release of French military prisoners and the end of hostilities.

According to the agreement made on the night of 10 April, the French forces left Urfa. The Armenians who were in the ranks of the French troops that were heading for Suruç shot at civilians. Upon this, the clans and the people came together and a violent battle started. At the end of this battle, which lasted for three hours, there were great loses on both sides, with a total of 296 people dying. Hearing about the incident, Ali Saip Bey came to the battlefield and saw that the French commander had been killed. The remaining 140 French soldiers were brought to Urfa as prisoners. On 11 April 1929, Urfa was finally free of the French, and this day is recognized as a day of independence for Urfa.

SECTION 2
HISTORICAL SITES

Harran Ulu Cami (Grand Mosque) Eastern Wall

1. THE CAVE WHERE PROPHET ABRAHAM WAS BORN

The cave where Prophet Abraham is believed to have been born lies to the east of Balıklıgöl (Fish Lake). Local tradition holds that Prophet Abraham was born in a cave south of the location of the courtyard of Dergah Mosque. According to this oral tradition, before Prophet Abraham was born, Nimrod ordered that all male babies

The cave where Prophet Abraham was born

were to be killed; to protect him, Abraham's mother gave birth in this cave. The cave is open to all visitors. The spring inside is believed to have curative qualities. Next to the cave is the Mevlid-i Halil Mosque, which was built in honor of Prophet Abraham's birth. This is a small mosque built in Ottoman times, and in 1986 a new one was built next to it, known as the Dergah Mosque.

2. THE PLACE WHERE PROPHET ABRAHAM WAS THROWN INTO THE FIRE, BALIKLIGÖL AND AYN-I ZELİHA

The place where Prophet Abraham was thrown into the fire and Balıklıgöl are both popular tourist sites. In fact, for many, these locations are the starting point of the tourist trail in Urfa. The area includes Urfa Castle, many mosques and historical sites.

Prophet Abraham called people to believe in one God, but they continued to worship the idols they were making. One day, when everybody was at a celebration, Prophet Abraham took an ax and destroyed all the idols, except for the largest one. He hung the ax around the neck of the last idol. When people returned, they said Abraham must have done this, as a lifeless object could not have performed such an act. Prophet Abraham was actually trying to show them how meaningless it is to revere manmade images that can bring neither good nor evil. The people were infuriated and Nimrod, the ruler, decided to punish Abraham by throwing him into a fire. The fire they prepared was so great that Abraham had to be launched into it by a catapult, for there was no other way to approach it. Then God Almighty ordered, "O Fire, be cool and peaceful for Abraham!" (Anbiya 21:69). Thus, the fire did not burn Prophet Abraham.

Balıklıgöl

Ayn-ı Zeliha Lake

According to popular belief, the fire turned into water and the wood into fish. The water that sprang from where Abraham had been thrown into the fire became a pond with fish, known as the Halilü'r-Rahman Lake or Balıklıgöl.

Rıdvaniye Mosque and its madrasa lie to the north of the lake. In the southwest corner of the lake, immediately next to where Abraham is believed to have fallen into the fire, are the Mosque of Halilü'r-Rahman and the madrasa. These buildings have become part of the scenery around the lake and together form a symbol for Urfa.

According to another popular tradition, Zeliha, the daughter of Nimrod, was one of those who believed in Prophet Abraham; as a result Nimrod punished her as well and threw her into the fire along with Prophet Abraham. Another spring appeared where Zeliha fell, and this also became a lake. This lake is now known as "Ayn-ı Zeliha," meaning "the spring of Zeliha," and is located to the south of Balıklıgöl. The fish in both these lakes are considered to be sacred and therefore are not touched.

There are documents that prove that Balıklıgöl has been in existence for a very long time, and it has often been mentioned by travelers in their writings. It is not known exactly when the spring here was turned into a lake, but tradition has it that this was done in 302 B.C. during the time of the Se-

❶ *The well where Prophet Job was cured*

leucids. The fact that there were fish in this lake and that they were considered to be sacred can be found in documents dating from that period.

3. THE CAVE WHERE PROPHET JOB SUFFERED AND THE WATER THAT CURED HIM

In this spot in the Eyyubiye district, which lies south of the Urfa city center, there is a cave where Prophet Job (Ayyub) was cured by water. Popular tradition has it that Prophet Job stayed in this cave for a very long time. When his afflictions had progressed to the extent that his tongue was affected and thus hindered his worship, he prayed to be cured. We are told in the Qur'an:

"And remember Our servant, Job, when he called out to his Lord: 'Surely Satan has caused me to be afflicted with distress and great suffering.' (We

The Cave of Prophet Jacob

never dried up. For centuries people have believed in the sacredness of this well and have turned to it for a cure. This is something that is found not only in Islam, but also in other religions as well. Bishop Nona, the religious leader of the Christians in Urfa, discovered in 460 C.E. that this water cured patients of leprosy.

4. THE WELL OF JACOB

The well of Prophet Jacob can be found in the Harran district of Urfa, to the north of the tomb of Hayat el-Harrani. It is said that Prophet Jacob lived in this area for a very long time. Prophet Abraham was married in Harran and after living there for some time, he migrated south. After his death, Jacob, who was Abraham's grandson, lived with his mother Rebecca near Jerusalem. Rebecca sent Jacob to Harran to find his uncles. It is said that Jacob met Rachel, his uncle's younger daughter, whom he would later marry, by a well in Harran. Jacob stayed in Harran for many years and had two sons with Rachel, Joseph and Benjamin. Today, the well that is known as the "Well of Jacob" is said to be the place where Jacob met Rachel.

told him:) 'Strike the ground with your foot: here is cool water to wash with and to drink.' We granted him his household and the like thereof along with them as a mercy from Us, and as a reminder (with guidance and instruction) for the people of discernment" (Sad 38:42–43).

Prophet Job dug the ground with his feet and found the water, drank from it and bathed in it. After a short while he was cured of his illnesses and recovered his health. It is said that the water which cured Prophet Job's illness still exists and that the well has

The Well of Prophet Jacob

The Ruins of the City of Prophet Shuayb

The Shrine of Prophet Elisha

5. THE CITY OF SHUAYB

This is an old city thirty kilometers (eighteen miles) to the east of the Harran district of Urfa, located in what is today the Özkent village. Only the remains of the city of Shuayb, where it is believed the Prophet Shuayb lived, can be seen now. A cave in the city is known as the station (maqam) of the Prophet Shuayb. This city, which is spread over quite a large area, is thought to date from the Roman era. The city was surrounded by walls, but today only some of the walls and foundations remain.

6. THE TOMBS OF PROPHETS JOB AND ELISHA (AL-YASA)

Twenty kilometers (twelve miles) from the Viranşehir district of Urfa is Eyyup Nebi village. The village takes it name from Prophet Job; the tombs of both Prophet Job and Prophet Elisha are believed to be located here. You can get here via the road that leads to Viranşehir—after eighty-five kilometers (fifty-three miles) follow the route that goes north, and the village is sixteen kilometers (ten miles) further on. In addition to the tombs of these two prophets, one can also visit the tomb of Rahime, the wife of Prophet Job.

As with those of other prophets, the burial places of these prophets were clouded by obscurity for a long time; their current locations were discovered under the direction of inspired religious scholars, or awliya. These graves were discovered during the reign of Murad IV. Returning from his Baghdad campaign, Murad IV stopped by Viranşehir and stayed there for a while. He had a dream about Prophet Job when he was there and this suggested to him that the grave of the prophet must be somewhere near. He then asked religious scholars and Sufi teachers in the region to find the grave. The place of the grave was indicated through spiritual signs and the burial places of both prophets were then turned into monuments.

7. THE WELL OF JESUS' HANDKERCHIEF

There is an ancient well in the Ulu Cami (Great Mosque) in Urfa. It is said that the well was there even before the Ulu Cami, which is almost a thousand years old, was built. According to oral tradition, the cloth that Jesus sent to the king of Edessa, Abgar V, is in this well. The cloth, which cured Abgar V's leprosy is believed to have fallen into the well; the water, which still exists today, is believed to have curative powers.

Another popular legend says that the cloth sent to Abgar V by Jesus was stolen by a thief and thrown into Jacob's well. A very strong light was emitted from the well at night and this helped people to find the cloth.

B. MOSQUES

After Urfa came under Muslim rule in 640, many mosques were built. Thirty–nine mosques are still standing today. Seven of these were built during the time of the Zengids, Ayyubids, and Akkoyunlus in the 12th, 13th, and 15th centuries respectively. The remaining 32 were built during Ottoman times. Apart from these,

there are also mosques that were converted from churches. There are seven different layouts in the mosques in Urfa. These are multi-pillar mosques, mosques where the central dome expands towards the sides, mosques with many equal-sized domes, ones with domed pulpits, single-domed cubic mosques, vaulted mosques and mosques that have been converted from basilicas.

All the traditional arrangements of Ottoman mosque architecture can be found in Urfa, except for two. These two are the reverse T-plan and the plan in which the central dome extends towards the sides with half domes.

Evliya Çelebi visited Urfa in the 1650's and he had the following to say about Urfa mosques in his travelogue: "There are 22 mosques in Urfa. In the inner castle there is the Minaresiz (without minaret) Mosque, which is an old temple. Near the Pasha's Palace there is the Kızıl Mosque, which has a large congregation. This was earlier a temple, dating from the time of Nimrod, but after the conquest, at the time of Harun Rashid, it was converted into a mosque. There are still organs in the minarets. Ak Cami Mosque is also a very old temple. Caliph Mamun first had the Halil Mosque built. The Pazar (Market) Mosque has a large congregation. Sultan Hasan, Ahaveyn and Debbağhane are also famous mosques. The Ibrahim Halil spring is carried over to these six mosques

and enlivens the fountains with abundant water. Other mosques are the Beykapısı Mosque, the Hekim Dede Mosque, the Karameydan Mosque, and the Uğurlu Meydan Mosque. This last one is also an old temple. There are around 67 mosques in different neighborhoods."

Some of the surviving mosques with historical interest are as follows:

1. ULU CAMİ

Ulu Cami is one of the oldest mosques in Urfa. The exact date of the construction of the mosque is not known, but it is estimated that it was built during the Zengid period, that is, between 1170 and 1175. It was renovated during the reign of Nureddin Zengi. There have not been any significant changes made to the building since that time.

It is reported that Ulu Cami was constructed on the ruins of a church.

View of the historical city from the minaret of Ulu Cami

Ulu Cami; the well in which the holy kerchief was thought to have fallen

The porticos of Ömeriye Mosque

The old church is thought to have been the church of Saint Stephanos, which was built at the beginning of the fifth century C.E. This mosque is also referred to as the "Crimson Church" due to its great number of red marble columns. It is said that some of the walls surrounding the courtyard of the mosque, some of the columns and column capitals were originally part of the Crimson Church. It is also said that the tower to the north of the courtyard, which is now used as the minaret, used to be the belfry of the church.

The minaret is octagonal and its circumference is the same as its height.

There is a well in Ulu Cami that dates back to ancient times. It is said that the well existed long before the mosque was constructed. According to oral tradition, a cloth that Jesus sent to Abgar V, the Edessan king, was thrown into this well. The cloth that cured Abgar fell into the well and as a result the water from the well is considered to have curative powers. There is still water in the Ulu Cami well.

2. ÖMERİYE MOSQUE

Ömeriye Mosque is situated near the Kazancı market, and it is one of the oldest mosques in Urfa. The exact date of the construction of the mosque is not known; however, on the eastern wall of the building, towards the back row of the congregation, there is an inscription that says the building was repaired in 1301.

The mosque has a rectangular plan with a dome in the middle; there are cross vaults running along the sides. The domes and vaults sit on columns that are partially imbedded in the walls and corners. On either side of the mihrab there are two balcony-like minbars in the front with free-standing columns, and at the back are two partially imbedded columns. The minbars are made of stone, with a half dome and they have iron latticework. The minbars of the Ömeriye mosque are the most intricate and finest examples of balcony minbars in Urfa.

3. THE MOSQUE OF HALİLÜ'R-RAHMAN

Ha The Mosque of Halilü'r-Rahman is situated at the southeast end of the Halilü'r-Rahman Lake, which is also known as Balıklıgöl. This is one of the oldest mosques in Urfa. To one side are a madrasa and a small graveyard. On the other side there is the *maqam* (station) which marks the place from where it is believed Prophet Abraham was thrown into the fire.

In the southeast corner of the mosque there is a stone minaret made from hewn stone; the minaret is square. The inscription on the minaret says that it was built on the order of Melik Eşref Muzaffereddin Musa of the Ayyubids in 1211.

Some sources say that the Halilü'r-Rahman Mosque was built on the site of the Church of Saint Mary, which stood here in Byzantine times. Prophet Abraham's maqam was built during the time of the Abbasid Caliph Ma'mun. Its shape is almost square and there are three platforms parallel to the mihrab.

Halilü'r-Rahman Mosque

4. SULTAN HASAN MOSQUE

Sultan Hasan Mosque was built by the sultan of the Akkoyunlu State, Uzun Hasan Bey, during the second half of the 15th century. It is a multi-domed mosque with a rectangular plan. The mosque is covered by three domes that rest on a wall facing the qibla. To the north of the courtyard there is a minaret with a polygonal body and a single balcony.

5. KADIOĞLU MOSQUE

The mosque was built in 1694 by Kadızade Hüseyin Pasha and is situated in the Kadıoğlu region of Su Meydanı. With its eight-columned structure, Kadıoğlu Mosque is a typical example of Ottoman mosque architecture. To the north of the courtyard is a cylindrical minaret that has a single balcony; this was constructed by the governor of Urfa Bahri Pasha in 1844. Because the lower part of the minaret is empty, Kadıoğlu Mosque is also known as the "Bottomless Minaret Mosque." In the courtyard is the Emencekzade Fountain, which was built in 1725.

6. NİMETULLAH MOSQUE (WHITE MOSQUE)

This mosque was built by the governor of Urfa Nimetullah Bey at the beginning of the 1500's. The plan is similar to that of the Edirne Üç Şerefeli Mosque. The gate to the mosque area is in the Ottoman portal style. On the northeast corner there is a cylindrical minaret with a single balcony. The minaret is one of the tallest in Urfa.

Rızvaniye Mosque

7. RIDVANİYE MOSQUE

This mosque lies to the north of Halilü'r-Rahman Lake. It was built in 1736 by the governor of Rakka-Urfa, Rıdvan Ahmet Pasha. When the mosque was being built, a madrasa was also built along the three sides of the courtyard of the mosque. The mosque has three domes along the mihrab wall, and it is of a rectangular plan. The door of the mosque is of the same date as the original construction. The woodwork on this door makes it unique among Urfa mosques. The wooden door is embossed and inlaid.

8. YUSUF PASHA MOSQUE

This mosque was built by Vezir Yusuf Pasha in 1709. The rectangular mosque is covered by six domes. The domes rest on two pillars in the middle and on the walls. In the eastern corner of the porticos, there is a cylindrical minaret with a single balcony. The mihrab is made of stone and has a remarkable geometric design. The minbar is decorated with similar ornaments carved out of stone in a style known as rumi.

Mevlid-i Halil Mosque

9. MEVLİD-İ HALİL MOSQUE

This mosque is situated near the cave in which Prophet Abraham is believed to have been born. This small mosque was built during Ottoman times in memory of Prophet Abraham and is known as Mevlidi Halil (The Birth of the Beloved Abraham). Its exact date of construction is not known. People who come to visit the cave can pray here, but as the mosque is too small to house many visitors, another mosque was built right next to it, known as the Dergah Mosque.

C. MOSQUES CONVERTED FROM CHURCHES

1. CİRCİS MOSQUE

Circis Mosque is situated near the market hall. It was built on the grounds of Martyr Sergius Church, which was built by Bishop Hiba in the fifth century. This church was destroyed twice by the Sassanids, in 503 and in 580, as well as being damaged many times in later years. When Saint Sergius Church was completely derelict, another church was built in the name of the martyr Saint Circis. In an inscription found in the mosque it is recorded that the building was completed in 1844 on the request of Abdülmecid Han. In the inscription next to the door it is written that the church was converted into a mosque in 1965 by Çarhoğlu Muhammed. After having been converted, the plan of the church was kept as it was, with a portico and a minaret being added to the north face.

2. FIRFIRLI MOSQUE

This mosque is known as the Fırfırlı (frilled) Mosque, situated

Salahaddin Eyyubi Mosque

on Vali Fuat Bey Street. The original name of this building is the Church of the Twelve Apostles; the date of the original construction is not known.

The entry door is on the western façade and is covered by a half dome; on the exterior the arches are pointed and pink marble has been used. The stonework, particularly on the western façade and the corner towers, is remarkable. This building was converted into a mosque in 1956; during the conversion one of the windows on the south wall was converted into the mihrab and the minbar was placed in front of the column that is imbedded in the middle of the south wall.

3. SALAHADDİN EYYUBİ MOSQUE

This mosque is situated on Vali Fuat Bey Street. Formerly, the Church of John the Baptist, built in 457 by Bishop Nona, stood here. The building was also used at one time as a courthouse. It is famous for its thirty-two red marble columns. It is believed that the structure that stands here today was built upon the remains of the Church of John the Baptist at the beginning of the eighteenth century, but later this too fell into disrepair.

The building remained in this state for a very long time, until being repaired in 1993 and reopened as Salahaddin Eyyubi Mosque.

D. CHURCHES AND MONASTERIES

1. DEYR YAKUB

Deyr Yakub is situated four kilometers (two-and-a-half miles) west of the cave of Prophet Job. Deyr Yakub sits on a high hill, and is locally referred to as the Throne of Nimrod. There is a mausoleum that belongs to the Aryu family, who were the descendants of the Edessan king

Deyr Yakub

Abgar Manu, which dates back to the first century B.C. The rectangular two-storey building that is adjacent to the mausoleum is thought to have been a monastery. In the first century B.C. idols were worshipped in the Edessan Kingdom. The monastery building was built during this time and it is believed that it was used as a temple for idols. During the time of Bishop Jacob of Serugh (Suruç) in the fifth century, the building was used as a monastery. This is thought to be the reason why this building is now referred to as Deyr Yakub (Monastery of Jacob). The sign of the cross inscribed on the large tomb suggests that this mausoleum was used as a grave for Christian kings.

2. THE CHURCH OF SAINT PETER AND SAINT PAUL (REGIE CHURCH)

This church is situated in the Nimetullah region of Urfa, around Ellisekiz Square. It was built by the Syrian Jacobites in 1861 and was dedicated to the disciples of Jesus, Saint Paul and Saint Peter. It forms a religious complex with the other buildings in the courtyard. Assyrians used to live in the district surrounding the church, which was used as a church and school until 1924, when the Urfa Assyrians migrated to Aleppo. The priest's lodgings are located in the north courtyard of the church.

After the emigration of the Assyrians from Urfa, this building was turned into a tobacco factory. After that it was used as a grape depot. Because it was used as a tobacco factory at one time, it is also now known as the "Regie Church." The building fell into disuse and was abandoned for many years. In 1997 it was restored by the Şanlıurfa Governor's Office and ŞURKAV (Şanlıurfa Culture and Art Education and Research Foundation). Today this building is used as the Vali Kemalettin Gazezoğlu Cultural Center.

The Church of Saint Peter and Saint Paul (Regie Church)

3. CHURCH OF THE NUNS

This building is situated in El-lisekiz Square, in the cul-de-sac that is east of Sheikh Safvet Dervish Lodge. The church resembles an Urfa house with an inner courtyard. It was built as a boarding house and church for traveling missionary nuns who came to Urfa in 1883.

E. TOMBS

1. ÇİFT KUBBE (DOUBLE DOME)

To the east of Şanlıurfa Castle is a graveyard situated on a hill. There are two domed tombs in the graveyard, but it is not known who is buried here. The tombs are called the "Double Dome," while the graveyard is known as the "Double Dome Family Cemetery." The two tombs, in the shape of cupolas, sit on eight supports. This style of tomb has been a model for many others in Urfa.

2. THE TOMB OF SEYYID HACI ALİ, THE SON OF SEYYID MAKSUD

The tomb of Seyyid Hacı Ali is situated in the Harran Gate graveyard. The tomb is known as the "King's Daughter" (Kral Kızı) tomb. The inscription states that it was built in November 1594. The tomb was constructed of hewn stone and sits on

Çift Kubbe (Double Dome)

an octagonal plan, covered by a single dome. In addition to Seyyid Ali, buried in the tomb are the Qadiri sheikh, Hacı Mustafa Efendi, who died in 1876, his three children, and Sheikh Huseyin, who died in 1969.

3. THE ZAVIYE (DERVISH LODGE) OF SHEIKH MESUD

The lodge was built on a hill to the west of the maqam of Prophet Job. This building is one of the oldest shrines in Urfa; it is built in the closed Seljuk madrasa style, with four vaulted rooms. One of the students of Hodja Ahmed Yesevi, Sheikh Mesud, is buried in the tomb. Sheikh Mesud was a great scholar and Sufi who played a major role in spreading Islam through Anatolia. In 1182, when the Ayyubids took control of Urfa there was a great migration from Turkistan to this area. Sheikh Mesud was one of these people who came to Urfa from Nishabour, near west Turkistan, with his students. After settling in Urfa, Sheikh Mesud had this building constructed in 1183. The lodge functioned as a madrasa, and lessons in Islamic jurispredence from the four Islamic schools were given in the four vaulted rooms. The students stayed in the caves that are situated to the southwest of the zaviye.

The empty coffin of Sheikh Mesud is in the room that lies to the east, while in the room below the vault is his grave. In the rooms below there are four more graves. These belong to Sheikh Mesud's sister and three of his students.

F. MILITARY ARCHITECTURE
1. ŞANLIURFA CASTLE (INNER CASTLE)

Şanlıurfa Castle is situated on a hill that is south of the Halilü'r-Rahman Lake (Balıklıgöl). The exact date of the original construction of the castle is not known; however, it is thought that it must have been built at the beginning of the 800's, during the Abbasid period. The east, west and south sides of İçkale (the Inner Castle) are surrounded by a deep defensive moat dug into the rock. The north face is solid rock. The castle was constructed on a rectangular plan, lying east to west and is built of hewn stone. The castle is built on a high hill at the southeast corner of the city walls, and it has played a significant role in the city's defense against enemies. The castle is surrounded on three sides by

The tomb and dervish lodge of Sheikh Mesud

pedestals of a great statue. The eastern column has an Assyrian inscription on it, which reveals that these columns were erected in the third century— before the construction of the castle— and that there was a large statue resting on them. This lost statue was built for the daughter of King Manu (who reigned in 240), Queen Salmet.

There are the remains of many structures in the castle that date back to the Byzantine and Islamic periods. There is a secret tunnel that runs from the top of the castle all the way down, and it is still in use today. The drinking water for the castle was carried through this tunnel from Ayn-ı Zeliha Lake.

a moat, making it difficult for it to be attacked. Throughout history many powerful armies had difficulty in conquering the castle.

There are two Corinthian columns in the castle. The local people call this the "catapult." However, it is understood that these originally acted as the

Urfa Castle has undergone many repairs since it was built. According to what we can understand from the inscription on the castle, it was repaired in 1462, during the reign of Uzun Hasan Bey, the sultan of the Akkoyunlu state, and then later, by the Karakoyunlu sultan Ebu'n-Nasr Hasan

Şanlıurfa Castle

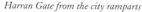

Harran Gate from the city ramparts

Bey Gate bastions from the city ramparts

Ali. Apart from this, it has also been documented that the castle was renovated in 921, 1048, 1548 and 1588.

2. CITY WALLS AND GATES

It is not known when the walls that surround the city were first built. But mention of these walls can be found in sources dating back to the seventh century C.E., revealing that they must have been built before that time. Most of the walls have been destroyed. What remains today are the Harran Gate, the Mahmudoğlu Castle that belongs to the Bey Gate, and some remains of the walls and other towers.

Some sources say that the city has eight gates. To the west is Sakıb's Gate, Su Kapısı (water gate), and West Gate, while to the northwest lies Samsat Gate and Palace Gate; to the

east are Bey Gate and Su Kapısı while Harran Gate is to the south.

G. MADRASAS

Some sources say that there were eighteen madrasas in Urfa in 1887. Some of these no longer exist today. Three important madrasas that have ceased to exist are the Ulu Cami Madrasa, the Hasan Padişah Camisi Madrasa and the Firuz Bey Madrasa. Like madrasas elsewhere in the Islamic world, the madrasas in Urfa were built around mosques as part of a complex. The following is some information about the madrasas that are still standing in Urfa today:

1. EYYUBİ (AYYUBID) MADRASA – THE MADRASA OF NAKİBZADE HACI İBRAHİM EFENDİ

The Ayyubid Madrasa was located to the east of Ulu Cami. Today this madrasa no longer exists; however its inscription panel, dating back to 1191, remains. In 1781 another madrasa, consisting of one room, was built on the location of the Ayyubid Madrasa. This madrasa, which is still standing, was built by Nakibzade Hacı Ibrahim Efendi and bears his name.

2. MADRASA OF HALİLÜ'R-RAHMAN

The Madrasa of Halilü'r-Rahman is situated to the west of Halilü'r-Rahman Lake (Balıklıgöl). The exact date of the construction of the madrasa is not known. There are rooms with porticos in front of the madrasa, and to the south of the lake there is a vaulted hall adjacent to the Halilü'r-Rahman Mosque. At the northwest corner of the lake there is a large, half-domed and barrel-vaulted room full of water. These buildings present an integrated complex with the mosque and the lake.

3. RIDVANIYE MADRASA

The Ridvaniye madrasa is situated in the courtyard of the Rıdvaniye Mosque, to the west of Halilü'r-Rahman Lake (Balıklıgöl). It goes round three sides of the mosque and was built in the same year as the mosque, in 1736, during Ottoman times. It was built by the governor of Rakka-Urfa, Rıdvan Ahmet Pasha, and bears his name. Porticos with a vaulted roof surround the madrasa rooms.

H. HAN (INN) BUILDINGS

There are eleven large hans that were built during Ottoman times. These are Gümrük (Customs) Han, Hacı Kamil Han, Barutçu Han, Mencek Han, Şaban Han, Kumluhayat Han, Fesadı Han, Samsat Kapısı Han, Millet Han, Bican Ağa Han and Topçu Han. There are also ruined hans including: Çifte Han, Aslanlı Han, Boyahane Han, Ali Bargut's Han, Zencirli Han, Cesur Han, Hacı Ali Ağa Han.

1. GÜMRÜK HAN

In the inscription panel above the door it is stated that Gümrük Han was built in 1562. Gümrük Han is also known as "Yetmiş Hanı" or as "Alaca Han" due to its two-colored stones. It is one of the most beautiful hans of Urfa, consisting of two floors built on a square plan. The han has a courtyard in the middle, and there are rooms surrounding the courtyard which function as shops. The second floor has a vaulted corridor running in front of the rooms. Above the entrance hall is the prayer room, or masjid. In 2001 Gümrük Han was partially restored.

2. MENCEK HAN

This is situated to the east of Pamukçu (Cotton) Market. The exact date of construction is not known. It has been estimated, according to information gathered from some sources, that it was built at the beginning of the eighteenth century. The outer façade is lined with shops. In the middle of the han is a square

Gümrük Han

Millet Han

Barutçu Han

Mencek Han

courtyard, which is also surrounded by shops. On the second floor of the han there are rooms surrounded by porticos with vaulted roofs.

3. MİLLET HAN

The date of construction of Millet Han, situated outside the Samsat Gate, is not known exactly. It was built outside the city gate as a rest stop for the caravans that came to town from different places. It is one of the biggest hans in Turkey with regards to the actual space it occupies. It has an expansive courtyard, and although there used to be a second floor, this no longer exists.

I. CARAVANSERAIS

As Urfa has always acted as the crossroads for important trade routes, great caravanserais were built on this road. The caravanserais that still exist today are: Han el-Ba'rür,

Çarmelik, Titriş and Mırbi (Ilgar). Han el-Ba'rür Caravanserai was built during the Ayyubid era, with the other three being built during the Ottoman period.

1. ÇARMELİK CARAVANSERAI

Çarmelik Caravanserai dates back to Ottoman times and can be reached by turning north (near the Regional Boarding School) forty-five kilometers (twenty-eight miles) along the Şanlıurfa–Gaziantep road and going another ten kilometers (six miles). Çar Melik means Four Sultans, and the caravanserai was given this name as it was built by four ruling brothers. It has a courtyard that measures 63 meters by 65 meters. Most of this caravanserai is in ruins.

2. HAN EL-BA'RÜR CARAVANSERAI

This caravanserai is twenty kilometers (twelve miles) from

Çarmelik Caravanserai

Han El-Ba'rür Caravanserai

Harran, in the village of Göktaş. Han el-Ba'rür Caravanserai was built during the Ayyubid period, in 1228 by al-Hajj Husamaddin Ali. The area it covers is 65 meters by 66 meters.

Some sections of this caravanserai, which is situated in the Tektek Mountain region, are in ruins. There are towers at the corners of the caravanserai. It was built around a large courtyard on a square plan. The caravanserai carries the characteristics of Anatolian Seljuk caravanserais and has a small mosque, a bath, and separate winter and summer quarters. The little mosque inside was restored in 1993 by the Şanlıurfa Governor's Office.

3. TİTRİŞ CARAVANSERAI

Titriş Caravanserai is in Titriş Village, in the Bozova district of Urfa. The exact date of construc-

tion is not known. The architectural characteristics of the caravanserai indicate that it is from the Ottoman period. The entrance to the caravanserai is through a gate that faces south. There are porticos on the east, west and north sides of the square courtyard. The roof on the northern side was later covered with concrete and the closed space that was behind it has been demolished to make space for new shops. The other three facades of the caravanserai have maintained their original appearance.

4. MIRBİ (ILGAR) CARAVANSERAI

This caravanserai is situated 35 kilometers northeast of the Birecik district, in the village of Mırbi (Ilgar). Mırbi Caravanserai was built at the crossroads of the Birecik-Diyarbakır and Birecik-Urfa caravan routes. The date of construction is not known; however, it is believed that

Titriş Caravanserai

Mırbi (Ilgar) Caravanserai

Hüseyniye Çarşıları

it dates back to Ottoman times. The caravanserai has a rectangular plan and is entered through the gate on the south side. In 1902–1903 a second floor was added to the caravanserai by Hartavizade Emin Ağa. Later Hartavizade Emin Ağa started to use the caravanserai as his residence. Today, the structure lies in ruins.

J. MARKETS

The markets that survive in Urfa today all date back to Ottoman times. The commercial inns and markets are mostly situated around Gümrük Han. The markets that remain today with their historical heritage are: Kazzaz Pazarı (Bedesten), Sipahi Pazarı, Koltukçu Pazarı, Pamukçu Pazarı, Oturakçı Pazarı, Kınacı Pazarı, Bıçakçı Pazarı, Kazancı Pazarı, Neccar Pazarı, İsotçu Pazarı, Demirci Pazarı, Çulcu Pazarı, Çadırcı Pazarı, Saraç Pazarı, Attar Pazarı, Tenekeci Pazarı, Kürkçü Pazarı, Eskici Pazarı, Keçeci Pazarı, Kokacı (Kovacı) Pazarı, Kasap Pazarı, Boyahane Çarşısı, Kavafhane Çarşısı, Hanönü Çarşısı, and Hüseyniye Çarşısı.

Urfa could easily be designated as the leading city in Anatolia for covered markets. Here it is appropriate to say a few words about these bazaars and markets.

1. HÜSEYNİYE MARKETS

Hüseyniye Markets consists of two covered markets that run parallel to one another. The covered markets lie between the Çadırcı Pazarı and Kazancı Pazarı and are both covered by fifteen colonnaded vaults; where the two markets meet the shops run back to back.

The market was built by Hüseyin Pasha, the son of Hartavizade Hafız Muhammed Selim Efendi. The keystone – on the northern façade of the market bears the inscription "Ma-sha Allahu Teala" (Whatever God Almighty Wills); on the left of the keystone is written "Nasrun min Allahi wa fathun qarib 1305." It can be translated as: "Help is from God and the victory is near." The year 1305 in the Islamic calendar corresponds to 1887.

Today the market is used by coppersmiths. The covered market that lies to the east was restored by ŞURKAV in 1998.

2. KAZZAZ MARKET (BEDESTEN)

Kazzaz Market was built adjacent to the south side of Gümrük Han in 1562. It runs west to east and has a cradle vault covered by four domes, back to back. The bedesten has four doors to the east, west, north and south. The shops in Kazzaz Market run along both sides, about a meter above the ground. The shops sell traditional Urfa clothing for men and women. Kazzaz Market was restored in 1999 by ŞURKAV.

3. SİPAHİ MARKET

Sipahi Market is a covered market adjacent to the west wall of the Gümrük Han. The market is a vaulted building, and there are many windows to let in the light. The shops of the market are built one meter above the ground and they are in two lines facing each other. The market is still in use today, and the shops sell items like carpets and kilims. The market has three gates. This historical market was restored by ŞURKAV in 1998.

K. BRIDGES AND AQUEDUCTS
KARAKOYUN STREAM AND BRIDGES

Karakoyun Stream (Daysan River) used to be a great river that ran through Urfa. It is known to have flooded three times in history and to have caused great damage. The three floods happened in 201, 413 and 525. These floods caused great destruction in the town and a great loss of life. After the flood in 525 the Byzantine Em-

Hacı Kamil Bridge

peror (Justinianus) had an embankment built on the Daysan River. This embankment is still standing. Out of the nine bridges built over the Karakoyun Stream, two have collapsed, while seven are still standing. These bridges, starting from Bey Gate are; Demirkapı Bridge, Beykapısı (Kısas) Bridge, Hacı Kamil Bridge, Eski Bridge (Samsat Köprüsü), Jüstinyen Aqueduct, Ali Saip Bey Bridge and Hızmalı Bridge.

The ones that have fallen into ruin are Demirkapı and Beykapısı Bridges. Hızmalı Bridge is on the Karakoyun Brook and it is not known exactly when it was built. From the inscription plaque on the eastern side of the middle support, we learn that repairs were carried out to it in 1843. This is one of the most beautiful bridges over the stream.

After some sections of the bridge collapsed in 2000, the Special Province Administration restored them. Millet Bridge provides the passage over the Karakoyun Stream to the Millet Hospital. After the stone banisters on the

Mahmud Nedim Efendi Mansion

Millet Bridge fell into ruin, they were restored by the Special Province Administration in 2001. The bridge has six high supports. The spaces between the supports have been completely filled with earth. Below the balustrade of the bridge there are little canals that carry water, and thus, the bridge also functions as an aqueduct.

L. VILLAS AND MANSIONS

1. MAHMUD NEDİM EFENDİ MANSION

This mansion was built in 1903 by Kürkçüzade Mahmud Nedim Efendi and is situated between Kehriz Street and Hastane Street in the Atatürk District. It has characteristics that recall European architecture; however, it also bears the stamp of traditional Urfa domestic architecture. Like many mansions, this one also has a haremlik (women's or family quarters) and selamlık (men's or visitors' quarters).

2. KÜÇÜK HACI MUSTAFA HACIKAMİLOĞLU MANSION

This mansion is situated on Vali Fuat Bey Street, across from the Salahaddin Ayyubi Mosque. It was built in the 1890's. The mansion fell into disrepair and was later restored by the governor's office in 1991. The mansion is built with Urfa stone and has haremlik and selamlık sections.

The selamlık section consists of two floors. The ground floor has "space for camels," a toilet and rooms for the servants. The second floor has rooms for guests. From the south side of the selamlık there is a passage to the haremlik. There is a courtyard with a fountain in the haremlik.

3. SAKIP'S VILLA

This villa is believed to have been built by the poet Sakıp Efendi in 1845, and it is situated in the Halepli Garden. It has haremlik and selamlık sections. It was restored in 1985 by the Şanlıurfa Municipality. The building is now used as the Headquarters of the Şanlıurfa Municipality Parks and Gardens Office. It consists of two floors and rests on a square plan. It has a courtyard, and to the west of the courtyard there is a hamam (Turkish bath).

M. TRADITIONAL URFA HOUSES

1. GENERAL CHARACTERISTICS

Traditional Urfa houses are surrounded by high walls and are two-storey structures made of stone. The streets between the houses are narrow with high walls. The second floors of the houses extend over the street.

The outer doors of the houses are either single- or double-winged and are made of smaller doors embedded in larger doors. There are a variety of shapes for the doorknockers. Some doors are zinc-plated.

Traditional Urfa houses usually consist of two sections, the haremlik and the selamlık. In some houses these two sections are separated by a wall, and the two sections become separate houses with separate doors. In some houses one enters the selamlık sec-

Sakıp's Villa

Akçarlar House (Harran University Culture House)

tion first through the front door and then passes into the haremlik section through a second door.

In the selamlık section there is usually a courtyard, a couple of rooms, an iwan, a stable for the guests' horses or camels and a toilet. The haremlik section is larger than the selamlık, and this is where the family members live. The kitchen, hamam and woodshed are located in the haremlik section. The windows of the haremlik look onto the courtyard. Usually, there is a little fountain, pool and well in the courtyard section of the house.

An iwan (or eyvan) is a vaulted hall open at one side. They create a cooler living space during the hot season, which is why these iwans are quite large.

In the basements are storerooms known as zerzembe. These cellars remain cool, and the locals use them as storage space for food that is prepared in summer for consumption in the winter. Urfa houses have large kitchens with 7–8 stoves, known as tandırlık.

2. EXAMPLES OF URFA HOUSES

a. Abdülkadir Hakkari House

Abdülkadir Hakkari House is in the Ulu Cami Neighborhood on Yorgancı Street, No: 16–18. The inscription over one of the doors suggests that it was built in 1866. It has a haremlik and a selamlık section, and consists of two floors. In the lower ha-

yat (entrance hall) there is a kitchen, woodshed, camel stable, zerzembe storage and a room. In the lower courtyard there are two staircases; one of these leads us up to the upper floor of the hayat and the other takes us to the summer quarters. On the north face of the summer quarters there is an iwan with two rooms on each side. There is a room and a stable in the entrance section of the selamlık. Via a staircase from the entrance to the selamlık one can reach the upper floor of the selamlık. In the middle of the selamlık there is an iwan, with a room on the east and another on the west side.

b. Akçarlar House (Harran University Culture House)

The exact date of construction for Akçarlar House, which overlooks Halilur Rahman Lake, is not known. Akçarlar House is one of the most beautiful houses in Urfa and it was restored between 1994 and 2001 by Harran University, being opened as the university's "culture house."

As with other houses, Akçarlar has selamlık and haremlik sections and a five-courtyard plan. It is built into a hill and on this side there are caves in the hill that are used as rooms. The house has two outer doors. From the door in the south one enters the selamlık section, and from the east, the haremlik section. There are two courtyards in the selamlık section, and the haremlik section consists of three courtyards on three different levels, all connected by staircases. On the ground floor of the selamlık there is a small courtyard, two rooms and a cave.

In the second courtyard on the ground floor there is a single room. When entering from the eastern door, one reaches the upper floor of the selamlık; this is connected to the first courtyard of the haremlik section. To the north of the courtyard there is an iwan that opens onto the courtyard and two rooms. On the other side are a kitchen and a fountain. On this floor there are also two large caves that are used as storerooms. From here one reaches the courtyard of the second floor via a staircase. This floor is used as the haremlik and there is a fountain in the middle. Another staircase leads into the third section of the haremlik, which again has a courtyard.

c. Akyüzler House

Akyüzler House, built in 1867, is to the east of Ellisekiz Meydanı (Square) on Tarakçılar Street. It has haremlik and selamlık sections. One enters the selamlık section through a large door and then a second door takes one to the haremlik section. The haremlik section has a square courtyard, and there are two floors running along the northern side of the courtyard. In the middle of both floors there is an iwan that opens onto the courtyard. Today, the roof of the second floor needs to be repaired, and therefore it is no longer in use.

d. Çardaklı Villa

Çardaklı Villa lies to the north of Halilü'r-Rahman Lake and its date of construction is not known. In 1992 it was bought by ŞURKAV and restorations started in 1997, being completed in 1999. Today, the villa is used as a restaurant. It consists of three floors. The reason why it is known as Çardaklı, or Pergola Villa is because each floor has a "pergola" room.

e. Hacı Bekir Pabuççu House

The date of construction of this house, one of the most beautiful houses in Urfa, is not known. The house is situated on 12 Eylül Street, and it consists of haremlik and selamlık sections. In 1980 the selamlık section was completely demolished. Like other Urfa houses, it is surrounded by high walls that separate it from the street. From the street gate one can enter the haremlik courtyard. To the south of the courtyard is a vaulted open space reminiscent of Seljuk madrasas. There is a fine pavilion above the rooms on the north side of the courtyard. On the façades surrounding the courtyard there is rich stonework. The woodwork in the rooms is also quite remarkable.

f. Hacı Hafızlar House

This house was built in 1888 by the famous Hacı Hafızlar family. The house is situated near Karameydan in the Izgördü Passage. It was bought by the Ministry of Culture in 1979 and restored, and now functions

Çardaklı (Pergola) Villa

Hacı Bekir Pabuççu House

Akyüzler House

Hacı Hafızlar House

as the State Fine Arts Gallery. It bears all the characteristics of an Urfa house and therefore is well worth visiting.

From the street the house can be accessed by two doors, one to the selamlık and the other to the haremlik. The door on the south side opens onto the selamlık section. The large room on the left in the selamlık section has an ornate façade on the courtyard side; there are three vaulted arches resting on round columns. To the north of the courtyard there is an iwan.

Through a door in the wall to the west of the selamlık courtyard one can access the haremlik section. The haremlik courtyard sits on a square plan and there is a flowerbed in the middle. There is also an iwan in the middle, with rooms on both sides. There is a third open-vaulted room in the haremlik courtyard, and there is a single domed hamam in the kitchen.

○ g. Hacı Imam Demirkol House

This house, No. 5 on Hacıban Street in the Cami Kebir District, was built in 1852 by Kürkçüzade Ahmet Bican Agha. Hacı Imam Demirkol House has some characteristics not found in other Urfa houses. One of these characteristics is that on the north and south faces of the courtyard there are summer and winter iwans. It has a well that has ornate stone carving. The revolving cabinet, which allowed women to serve guests without being seen by men, is connected to the vestibule.

N. URFA MUSEUM

Şanlıurfa Museum is an exhibition space in which one can see artifacts from the different historical periods of the town. There are items that date back to 9000 B.C. from Göbekli Hill, and items also from the more recent past, with an array of objects spanning the eleven-thousand-year history of Urfa. In the courtyard of the museum are mosaics from the Roman and Byzantine periods and several stone statues from various other historical periods of the town. Indoors, the museum has three halls.

The first hall on the ground floor displays items from Assyrian, Babel and Hittite periods. Among them is the stele from Harran, from the period of the Babylonian King Nabonid. On this stele Nimrod is depicted praying to gods moon, sun and star. In the second and third halls of the museum one can see artifacts dating back to the Neolithic Age (7250–5500 B.C.), sharp objects made of flint, stone idols and pans. There are also painted and plain ceramics made of baked clay, seals, pithos and necklaces from the Chalcholitic Age. (5500–3200 B.C.). From the Old Bronze Age (3200–1800 B.C.) one can see a seal stamped earthenware jug, cylindrical and stamp seals, earthenware animal figurines, metal objects, jewelry and idols. On the upper floor of the museum one can see costumes from the region, silver and bronze jewelry, ornate wooden doors and windows purchased from Urfa houses, calligraphy compositions, handwritten Qur'ans and glassware.

Urfa Museum

SECTION 3
SIGNIFICANT DISTRICTS AND SITES TO VISIT

Harran Castle

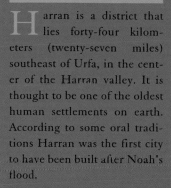

A. HARRAN

Harran is a district that lies forty-four kilometers (twenty-seven miles) southeast of Urfa, in the center of the Harran valley. It is thought to be one of the oldest human settlements on earth. According to some oral traditions Harran was the first city to have been built after Noah's flood.

It is believed that the place that is referred to as "Haran" in the Old Testament is Harran. The name of Harran appears on cuneiform tablets found in Kültepe and Mari, which date back to 2000 B.C., where it is recorded as Har-ra-na or Ha-ra-na. According to some sources, the name Harran comes from the word Haran or Aran, the name of Prophet Abraham's uncle. Historical documents attest to the fact that Harran's name has remained unchanged since 4000 B.C. According to some, the name Harran comes from the Sumerian or Akkadian word Haran-u, meaning "traveling caravan," while others say that it means crossroads. It is also claimed that the word Harran comes from the Arabic word harr, which means very hot.

According to Islamic historians, Harran was the center of upper Mesopotamia. Harran is situated at the crossroads of important trade routes that come from northern Mesopotamia; they meet here and are linked to the west and the northwest. Trade from Anatolia to Mesopotamia and from Mesopotamia to Anatolia has traveled through Harran for thousands of years. Consequently, Harran is a city that bears the traces of various cultures and great civilizations. But first and foremost, Harran is known as the land of Prophet Abraham; according to some oral traditions Prophet Abraham was born in Harran and, as stated above, his uncle was called Harran. Another oral tradition states that Prophet Abraham stopped in Harran when traveling to Palestine, staying here awhile. There is a mosque that bears Abraham's name here. According to some Qur'anic commentators, the land mentioned in the Qur'anic verse, "And We delivered him (Abraham) as well as Lot (removing them) to the land which We had blessed for all people" (Al-Anbiya 21: 71) is Harran.

Idolatry was common in Harran starting with the Assyrians, Babylonians and Hittites until the eleventh century C.E. The idolaters who resided in Mesopotamia worshiped the moon, the sun and the planets. Harran was, for a very long period of time, the center of idolatry and Christians called it Helle-nopolis, meaning the city of Hellenes or Greeks, a people who had become synonymous with idolatry. Even after the advent of Islam, idolatry contin-ued in the region. Under Islamic rule, the idolaters were allowed to carry out their religious rituals.

Harran University is famous as the world's first university, and it has con-tinued to exist throughout the ages, pro-ducing many world-famous scholars. The great mathematician and doctor Thabit ibn Qurra, Al-Battani, who was the first to calculate the correct distance between the earth and the moon, and Jabir ibn Hayyan, the first scientist to claim that the atom was divisible, were leading scholars who were educated at Harran. There are three schools of phi-losophy, the Athenian, the Alexandrian and then the Harran school. Philoso-phers educated in Harran were famous throughout the world.

Harran became a part of the Is-lamic lands in 640, and was made the capital of the Umayyad State in 744 by Marwan II. During the Abbasid Harun Rashid period, Harran Uni-versity had a great reputation in the Islamic world and students came here from all over the world.

1. SITES IN AND AROUND HARRAN

a. Harran Houses

Harran houses are remarkable for their conical roofs. All of these houses are now protected by a cultural heritage program. The Har-ran houses were built over the last

150–200 years, using material from the antique structures that lie in ruins around the area. The houses are built on a square plan.

The single domes that are adjacent to one another are linked inside by arches, thus creating spacious living quarters. If one takes into account the climate of the region, the fact that these houses are cool in the summer and warm in the winter explains the importance of this architectural design.

b. Harran University

The date of the university's establishment is not known; however, it is known that the university functioned in the first centuries after Jesus; this institution is also famous as one of the most important schools of philosophy in the world. The third most important school of philosophy, those of Alexandria and Athens, is Harran. The university continued to function after Harran was conquered by the Islamic armies. From 718 to 913, when Harran was part of the Islamic territory, the town reached its zenith in science and art, and Harran was the home of many world-renowned scholars. At the time, many students from all over the Islamic world came to study here. Muslim, Christian, Sabean, and pagan scholars worked in harmony at this university.

Ulu Cami, which lies to the northeast of the Harran Mound is usually mistakenly described as Harran University, so the minaret of the mosque is mistaken for a watchtower. However, there is no information in any historical source that this was the university. Today, no remains of Harran University have been identified and its exact location is unknown.

c. City Walls

Some of the four kilometer-long (two-and-a-half miles) city walls which surround Harran still remain today. The walls have 187 towers and they are very sturdy, made of hewn stone. There used to be eight gates in the walls. The Aleppo Gate remains standing today. The walls used to be surrounded by a moat, but now it has been filled in with earth.

d. Harran Castle O

Harran Castle lies to the southeast of the city. The exact date of the construction of this castle, which is adjacent to the city walls, is unknown. It is said that the castle was built on the site of a Sabean temple. Harran Castle was used as the palace of the ruler in various periods. It consists of three floors, but today is in a partially ruined state. The castle is surrounded by moats, which are lined with stones. The castle was renovated in 1059 by the Fatimid state.

e. Ulu Cami ⦿

Ulu Cami (Great Mosque) lies to the northeast of the Harran Mound. The mosque was first built in 640 when the Islamic armies conquered Harran. Ulu Cami was renovated by the Umayyad sultan Marwan II from 744 to 750. In some sources, this mosque is referred to as Cami el-Firdevs (the Mosque of Paradise) or "The Friday Mosque." The mosque is built on the site of the Sin (Great Moon) Temple of the Sabeans, which existed in the Roman period. When the Umayyad General Iyadh ibn Ghanam took the town, he had the temple demolished and gave the Sa-

beans another plot of land on which to build their temple. The mosque fell into disrepair, but in 1174 it was restored by Nureddin Zengi in an elaborate manner.

Harran Ulu Cami is one of the oldest and largest mosques in Anatolia and has the best stone embellishments. The mosque has nineteen doors. There used to be a fountain in the courtyard, and one could enter this space from three different doors, east, north and west. From behind the qibla wall there was a staircase which led to the pulpit (mihrab). The mosque was divided into four sections with three columns standing parallel to the pulpit. The mosque did not have a dome, but rather was covered by a wooden roof, which collapsed after a fire.

Today, the east wall of the mosque, with its inscription plaque, the qibla

wall, the pulpit, the middle arch inside the mosque and the square minaret are still standing. This minaret, which is only partially standing, rises to the east of the north wall, standing 29 meters. There are also many decorated column heads and arched stones remaining from the original structure.

f. The Tomb of Sheikh Hayat al-Harrani

Hayat Al-Harrani lived in the twelfth century. He was a great Islamic scholar and Sufi. He died in 1185, and this tomb was built in 1195 by his son. The tomb lies to the west of the city, outside the city walls. Before Sheikh Hayat al-Harrani's death there was a small mosque standing next to his house. The mosque is adjacent to the tomb on the southern side. It is said that the place is also the burial site of Abraham's father, Azar. The mosque and the tomb were restored from 1999 to 2001 by the General Directorate of Foundations.

g. Harran Höyüğü (Harran Mound)

Harran Mound is in the middle of the town, south of the Ulu Cami. It was first discovered in excavations in 1951. First the castle and its surrounding area and then the region around the Firdevs (Ulu) Cami were cleared. The Harran Mound revealed various artifacts dating from as far back as 3000 B.C. up to the thirteenth century C.E. Among these is a stele belonging to the Babylonian King Nabonid. Also, ceramics and coins from the Umayyad, Ayyubid and Seljuk periods were found here.

In addition to these, many earthen

Sheikh Hayat el-Harrani's Tomb

Harran Tumulus

figurines, stone weights, millstones and bronze items have been found. Coins from the Islamic period, many precious ceramics, both glazed and painted, have also been found; all of these are on display at the Urfa museum.

There are structures dating back to the Islamic periods, from seventh to the thirteenth centuries on the Harran tumulus. These remains provide us with information about the Islamic architecture of that period. Not only do some of the houses have wells in their courtyards, but also there are wide streets that have wells in the middle. The city seems to have been spread over a large space, and it had a sewer system, toilets on platforms with lids, bathing rooms, mills and produce depots. The ruins of this organized and planned city show the level of civilization in Harran at that time.

h. Sin Temple

Sin Temple of the Babylonians in Harran is mentioned as one of the oldest temples on tablets that date back to 2000 B.C. Sin was the name of the moon god. The exact place of this temple is not known, however, it is thought that it was near the location of Ulu Cami or the tumulus. In some sources this temple is mentioned as being in the location of Ulu Cami; it is said that after the Muslims seized Harran they destroyed the temple and built the mosque on its site. The idolaters were shown another place to build their temple.

2. EMINENT PERSONS WHO LIVED IN HARRAN

a. Sheikh Yahya Hayat al-Harrani (d. 1185)

The sheikh's full name, which reflects his lineage, is Yahya Hayat ibn Qays ibn Rajjal (Rahhal) ibn Sultan al-Ansari al-Harrani. As the sheikh's roots stretch back to the Ansar, the residents of Medina at the time the Muslims arrived from Mecca, he is also known as Ansari. Sheikh Yahya Hayat al-Harrani was born in Falluja, and he then came to Harran to live, dying here.

Sheikh Yahya Hayat al-Harrani was a great spiritual figure. When an oath was to be taken on an important matter, it was taken in his name. There is no clear information about the date of birth, the family or the education of Hayat al-Harrani. He is believed to have been born at the start of the twelfth century. This eminent scholar spent fifty-five years of his life in Harran and he acted as imam in the mosque that is now adjacent to his tomb, where he taught many students. He is also known as one of the four great sheikhs whose spheres of providence span not only their lifetime, but also the time after their death as well. According to oral tradition, these four sheikhs are Maruf al-Karhi, Abdulqadir al-Jilani, Uqayl al-Manbiji and Hayat al-Harrani.

Hayat al-Harrani was a Sunni Muslim of the Hanafi School, and was a Naqshbandi Sufi. Harranis

Tomb of Sheikh Hayat el-Harrani

would call him as mediator when they wanted to pray for rain. He was a good-humored and generous man. Hayat al-Harrani was devoted to supererogatory prayers and lived a life of seclusion. Important personages of his era would visit him, receiving and partaking in his blessings. Among these people were Nureddin Zengi and Saladin Ayyubi. Hayat al-Harrani died in Harran in 1185, when he was around eighty years old. His tomb is located to the west of Harran, outside the city walls. There is a mosque adjacent to the south of the tomb.

Here it would be appropriate to quote some of Hayat al-Harrani's words of wisdom that reflect his love of God:

"The lover is impatient to reach the beloved. In the heart, there is a great sadness made up of fears. Dear beloved! I am crossing the desert on foot. All the valleys and mountains that I come across direct me constantly to you."

There are some miraculous stories attributed to Hayat al-Harrani. According to some oral reports there were times when there would be no water on the Harran plain for days. The people would ask Hayat al-Harrani for his blessing to pray for rain. After performing these prayers the rains would come, and he would be considered as having acted as a means to help them attain the blessings of God.

The sheikh is said to have performed other wonders (karama) like this. Once he had a disagreement with a mason about the direction of the qibla in a mosque that was being built. The sheikh asked the man to look at the ground. The man saw the Ka'ba before him and fainted in terror at this phenomenon. Another wonder is reported by Najiduddin of Harran:

"Hayat al-Harrani was on his way to Hajj. One day he stopped and his servant told him, 'Master, I long for some fresh dates.' The sheikh says, 'Shake this tree.' The servant says, 'But this is not a date tree; it is just a bush.' The sheikh insisted, 'Just shake it.' The servant shook the tree and fresh dates started to fall. All the people there ate until they were full."

Such occurrences continued after his death as well. Here we would like to present some recent examples:

When a group of visitors arrived in Urfa, a great religious scholar advised them to go to Harran to visit Hayat al-Harrani. The visitors agreed to go; when they came to the tomb the imam asked, "Are you followers of Risale-i Nur?" and the surprised group said they were. The imam of the mosque said, "Welcome. I knew you would come. Last night Sheikh Hayat al-Harrani appeared in my dream and he said, 'I will have visitors tomorrow, receive them well!' This is the order of my master" (Risale-i Nur is a Qur'anic exegesis written by Bediüzzaman Said Nursi).

A man who worked at a students' boarding house in 1995 in Harran said that when he was working at night he often saw Hayat al-Harrani come to the house and pull the blankets over the sleeping students.

Again in the 1990's Yusuf Bey from Izmir came to visit Hayat al-Harrani's tomb. Yusuf Bey is a Turkish man who has provided great service to his country, who has spent his life working in various religious services in Izmir; he then moved onto the Central Asian republics to devote his life to the education of the people there. Yusuf Bey visited the tomb with a friend. The keeper of the tomb at the time was a certain Mehmet Ali. Seeing the visitors arrive, Mehmet Ali jumped to his feet and went outside. When he was asked why had done this, he replied, "Didn't you see? The sheikh stood up." He also knew the names of the visitors, although he had never seen them before.

b. Thabit ibn Qurra

Thabit ibn Qurra lived in Harran from 821 to 901 and educated himself in the fields of philosophy, mathematics, astronomy and the natural sciences, writing works in these fields. He also did some famous translations from Greek. He can be said to be one of the two great Islamic translators. He wrote around 150 works in Arabic and fifteen works in Assyrian. He wrote books and developed theories in all fields of mathematics. Thabit ibn Qurra wrote a book on the movements of the sun that are visible to the naked eye. He was one of the best-known doctors in the East during his lifetime. He also wrote many musical works.

c. Abu Abdullah al-Battani

Abu Abdullah al-Battani lived from 858 to 929 and worked in the fields of astronomy and mathematics. He had intricate knowledge of the stars. He was one of the first people to devise theorems on algebra and geometry, and he was well known in the West as well. He worked in an observatory he set up in Rakka for forty-two years. His calculations for the lunar eclipse were correct, and so were his measurements of the lengths of seasons and the movements of the sun. His observations about solar and lunar eclipses were the sole source of information and criteria up until the end of the eighteenth century. He can be considered to be one of the most important figures to have contributed to astronomy.

d. Sinan ibn Thabit

Sinan ibn Thabit was the son of Thabit ibn Qurra and the chief physician at the Baghdad Hospital. He educated and supervised the doctors who worked there. He wrote many books on medicine, astronomy, geometry and literature. He was very well versed in numbers, geometry, and medicine. He also carried out some studies in the field of history. He wrote a book that covered the history of the world, starting from the beginnings of the world to his own day. He died in 943 in Baghdad.

e. Abu Ishak Ibrahim ibn Hilal as-Sabii

Abu Ishak Ibrahim ibn Hilal as Sabii was born in 925 in Harran and he was one of the most famous authors of his time. He was known for his writings, rhetoric and poetry. He was trained in medicine by his father. He completed his first education in Harran and then came to Baghdad, where he concentrated on Arabic language and literature. He also wrote works on mathematics and geometry. He died in 994 in Baghdad.

f. Ibn Taymiyya

Ibn Taymiyya was born in Harran and belonged to the Hanbali school of thought. He lived in Damascus from 1261 to 1327 after the Mongol invasion. In addition to Qur'anic exegesis, hadith and fiqh (Islamic law), he also worked in the field of mathematics. He is known for his work on kalam (Islamic theological philosophy) and philosophy.

B. VİRANŞEHİR
1. THE HISTORY OF VİRANŞEHİR

Because this city was destroyed many times in history, it became known as viran, meaning "in ruins." It is believed that there has been a city here since 2750 B.C. The city is situated on the historic silk route, which caused it to be a target for attacks from the third century B.C. to the sixteenth century C.E. With its fertile land, it was an important city in upper Mesopotamia. In 1900 B.C. it was a Hittite city, while in 1115 B.C. it became Assyrian, being re-annexed by the Hittites in the fourth century B.C. In 163 B.C. it fell into Roman hands and after that the

Viranşehir Martyrion Ruins

Persians took control of Viranşehir.

The city continued to change hands between the Romans and the Iranians until 622 C.E., after which date it was conquered by Islamic armies. After 660 the city fell to the Hamdanis, and then became part of the Abbasid State in 894. During the rule of Melikşah it was under the rule of the Seljuks, changing hands between the Byzantines, Seljuks, Arabs, Iranians and Artuks in subsequent years. In 1071 Viranşehir was once again Seljuk, and in 1108 the Artuks reclaimed it. In 1202 the city was taken by Nureddin Zengi, the Atabey of Mosul.

Viranşehir was destroyed by Hulagu Khan in 1258. In 1400 it was destroyed once again by Timur. This second destruction was complete, and no stone was left standing. In 1516, during the rule of Yavuz Sultan Selim the city became part of the Ottoman Empire and Viranşehir was made part of Diyarbakır. Since 1924 it has been an administrative district of Şanlıurfa.

Shrine of Prophet Job

Shrine of Prophet Elisha

2. IMPORTANT SITES IN VİRANŞEHİR

T he important sites in Viranşehir are the tombs of Prophet Job, Prophet Elisha, and Rahime, the wife of Job.

a. Temple Columns

O ne of the most important edifices in this town is the Temple Columns of the old town. These are also know as the "Dikmeler" and are part of the Octagonal Temple from the Roman period. The temple has been completely destroyed except for these two great columns.

b. The Tombs of Prophets Job and Elisha

T he tomb of Job is located in Eyyub Nebi Village in the Viranşehir district. When you go to Viranşehir from Urfa, the road for the tomb turns north at the 85th kilometer (53rd

Çimdin Castle

mile), and the tomb is about fifteen minutes from here. This is a village of prophets. The shrines of Prophet Job, Prophet Elisha, and Rahime, the wife of Job are located here.

c. Çimdin Castle

This is a castle that lies fifty kilometers (thirty-one miles) northeast of Soğmatar. It can be reached by turning south at the sixty-first kilometer (thirty-eigth mile) of the Urfa-Mardin road; it is a further nine kilometers (five-and-a-half miles) up the road. The castle was built on a large hill and it was constructed by the Ayyubids for defense purposes in 1182–1239. It is surrounded by a moat on all sides.

C. BİRECİK

Birecik is a district that lies eighty kilometers (fifty miles) west of Urfa. It is built on the banks of the Euphrates, and thus has always held an important position throughout history. The name Birecik comes from the Aramaic word birsa, meaning castle.

Its situation on the banks of the Euphrates makes the town very fertile. There are many olive and hazelnut groves here. Many farms also raise livestock, and fruit and vegetables are grown in great abundance.

In Birecik one can see bald ibises, now an endangered species. They are found only in North Africa and Birecik. These birds are called "kel" or "bald" because they have no feathers on their heads or necks. They are 70–75 cm tall and they live in the rocky regions of Birecik. Visitors can see them in their protected habitat.

1. HISTORY OF BIRECIK

Birecik is a town that is as old as humanity itself. It is considered

Birecik Castle

to be one of the centers around which humans began agricultural life. It is estimated to have a history of between eight and nine thousand years.

In 2000 B.C. Birecik belonged to the Hittites. After that, in 840 B.C., it fell to the Assyrians, and then to the Persians, the Macedonians, the Romans, and then to the Byzantines. It was conquered by the Islamic armies in 640, under the leadership of Caliph Umar.

After remaining part of the Great Seljuk State for a while, Birecik came under the rule of the Byzantines in 1096. After this brief Byzantine rule the town fell into the hands of the Artuks, then the Ayyubids, Mamluks, Akkoyunlu and Karakoyunlu states. From 1098–1150, it was a crusader fortress. After the thirteenth century and up till the fifteenth, the city was under the rule of Syrian Mamluks. Af-

ter that, during Yavuz Sultan Selim's Egyptian campaign in 1516, it became part of Ottoman lands, and remained under Ottoman rule for centuries, enjoying a peaceful existence.

During the War of Independence, Birecik was occupied in 1919 first by the English and then by the French. During these years the people of Birecik put up great resistance and thousands of people lost their lives. The occupying forces left the town on 19 July 1920. After the construction of a long bridge over the Euphrates river in 1956 Birecik became an important crossroads.

2. HISTORICAL SITES

a. Birecik Castle (İçkale)

Birecik Castle is built on a high rock near the Euphrates river. It is also called the İç (inner) or Beyaz

(White) Castle, and it is thought to have existed since 2000 B.C. The castle has been rebuilt many times since that date and it took on its present form in the thirteenth century C.E.

The foundations of Birecik Castle, situated on a hill, are 36 meters above the surrounding land. The total height of the castle, including the hill, is 60 meters. As the east and northeast sides of the castle are high, the moat has turned the castle into an island. This characteristic has made the castle a good stronghold for Birecik during times of attack. The castle has three floors and there were originally twelve turrets. However, only one of these turrets remains. When the Mongolians invaded Birecik they destroyed everything, yet they did not manage to conquer the castle.

b. City Walls (Outer Castle) ⚙

Birecik was established to the east of the Euphrates River, with the west of the city being guarded by the river. The other three sides are surrounded by walls and thus all four sides are protected. All the towers, turrets, and gates of these walls are fortified. The walls, which are for the most part in ruins, have four gates: Meydan Gate, Urfa Gate, Meçan Gate and Bağlar Gate. The last restoration of the city was made during the Mamluk period by Sultan Kayıtbay in 1478.

c. Ulu Cami ⚙

Ulu Cami is situated in the Merkez District, İskele Çarşısı (Market). It is not known for certain when the mosque was built or

by whom. On an inscription plaque on a door in the mosque it is stated that it was built in 1802. However, it is believed that the mosque was built much earlier than the plaque states, and that the plaque actually refers to a restoration rather than the original construction. It is architecturally similar to the Urfa Ulu Cami. When one takes these architectural characteristics into consideration it can be deduced that this mosque must have been built in the twelfth century. The mosque has a multi-dome rectangular plan and it sits on twelve supports.

D. OTHER HISTORICAL SITES IN URFA

1. CABİR EL-ENSAR MOSQUE AND TOMB

This mosque and tomb are situated twenty kilometers (twelve miles) north of Harran, in the Yardımcı Village. It is said that the tomb belongs to one of the Companions of Prophet Muhammad, Jabir ibn Abdullah and that he came with the army that was sent to conquer the region. However, Jabir ibn Abdullah himself is not buried here, but rather a severed limb. Near the tomb is a mosque that carries the same name. The mosque originally had three domes, with the fourth being added later. The stone carvings are considered to be unique in Urfa.

Jabir ibn Abdullah was born in 607 in Madina. His father was one of the martyrs of Uhud, Abdullah ibn Amr. Jabir was the youngest among the group at Aqaba to swear allegiance to Prophet Muhammad. After Uhud, he took part in all the wars. He is one of the Companions to have related the largest number of hadiths. He also fought in wars after the death of Prophet Muhammad. Jabir was in the army that conquered Damascus. It is believed that after that he was

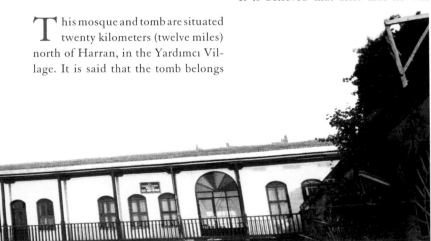

Imam Bakır Mosque

also present at the conquest of Urfa and Harran and that a part of his body is buried in this tomb. The mosque and the tomb were restored in keeping with the original structure.

2. IMAM BAKIR MOSQUE AND TOMB

I mam Bakır Mosque and tomb are situated in Imam Bakır Village, three kilometers (1,8 miles) to the northeast of Harran. This tomb belongs to the fifth imam of the twelve Shiite imams, Abu Jafar Imam Muhammad Bakır. Both parents of Imam Bakır were descendants of Fatima al-Zahra (the daughter of Prophet Muhammad). He was born in 676 in Medina. When he died in 721, he was buried in Medina. However, during the period of Caliph Umar he participated in the conquest of Urfa and Harran, and during the battle he lost a finger. A tomb and a mosque were built at the place where the finger was buried.

3. HAN AL-BA'RÜR CARAVANSERAI

T his is a caravanserai located twenty kilometers (twelve miles) from Harran in Göktaş Village. Han

al-Ba'rür Caravanserai was built during the time of the Ayyubids, by al-Haj Husameddin Ali, in 1228. The caravanserai is situated in the Tektek Mountain region, and some parts of it are in ruins. There are towers at the corners of the caravanserai, and it was built around a big square courtyard. The caravanserai is characteristic of the Anatolian Seljuks, and it has a mosque, bath, summer and winter quarters. The mosque was restored and decorated by the Urfa Governor's office in 1993.

4. THE RUINS OF THE CITY OF SHUAYB

T hese ruins are to be found thirty kilometers (eighteen miles) east of Harran, in Özkent Village. They are known as Shuayb Şehri (City of Shuayb). It is thought that these ruins date back to the Roman period. This city is spread over a large area and is surrounded by walls. It has been completely ruined except for some walls and foundations. The city is known

by this name because it is thought that the Prophet Shuayb lived here. The cave in the city is known as the maqam of the Prophet Shuayb.

5. THE SOĞMATAR RUINS

These ruins are situated sixteen kilometers (ten miles) north of the City of Shuayb, in the Yağmurlu Village. Soğmatar is a historical town that dates back to the times before Jesus, and it is believed that Prophet Moses lived here and had a farm here. According to popular belief, after leaving Egypt, Moses came here and touched the ground with his staff; as a result the well that is now known by his name miraculously appeared. According to another popular narrative, Moses met the daughters of Shuayb here. He helped the girls at this well, watering their sheep and then the girls took him to their father. He married one of the girls and he lived in this region for a while.

The Ruins of the City of Shuayb

Soğmatar was a center for idol worship during the Assyrian and Babylonian periods. According to this pagan belief, the moon, the sun and the planets were considered to be holy. At "Holy Hill," situated south of the castle, there is an open-air temple dedicated to the chief god of this religion. On this hill there are relief works depicting the gods.

There are seven temples to the west and north of Holy Hill. It is believed that these temples were dedicated to the Sun, the moon (Sin), Saturn, Jupiter, Mars, Venus and Mercury. The Sabeans in Soğmatar used to pray and perform ritual slaughters in these temples.

The Pognon cave in the town is famous for its human figures in relief that represent gods. These relief works are believed to have been made in 150–200 B.C. and there is an Assyrian inscription beside them.

6. SENEMIGAR (SANEM CAVE)

This cave is situated eleven kilometers (seven miles) north of Senem Mığar Village. There is a building consisting of three floors standing on a hill. It is believed that this structure dates back to the fifth century and that it was either a monastery or a palace. It is also said that the region was an important center for Christianity in the early years. There are churches carved into the rocks in this town, and the rock tombs here are also quite remarkable.

SECTION 4
IMPORTANT PERSONAGES

Eyyub Nebi Village, Patience Stone

1. PROPHET ABRAHAM (İBRAHİM)

Prophet Abraham was a great prophet; he is considered to be the forefather of the three Abrahamic religions, Judaism, Christianity, and Islam. The lineage of many prophets whose names are mentioned in the Qur'an can be traced back to him, the chief among these being Moses, Jesus, and Muhammad. All revelatory religions accept that he had a great character and was very virtuous.

Prophet Abraham is the second most frequently mentioned prophet in the Qur'an after Moses, being mentioned sixty-nine times. The Qur'an describes Abraham as a role model and demands that his religion and example be followed. This is reflected in the following verse: "Indeed, you have had an excellent example to follow in Abraham and those in his company" (60: 4) as well as in another one: "Say: God has spoken the truth, therefore follow the religion of Abraham, the upright one; and he was not one of the polytheists." (3: 95). One of the most frequently praised qualities of Abraham in the Qur'an is his submission to God (22: 78; 2: 131, 16: 120–121); that is, he submitted to all of God's orders without question. In the Qur'an Abraham is described as an upright man (19: 41), a man who is thankful for God's gifts (16: 120–121), who is sound of heart (37: 84), who is merciful and gentle-natured (9: 114), who continually asks for forgiveness, and who has devoted himself to God (11: 75, 9: 114).

Prophet Abraham is also known as "the father of guests" and "the master of youth." One of his attributes in the Qur'an is Khalilullah (the friend of God). In one verse it is said, "God has taken Abraham as friend," (4: 125) indicating the relationship between the two. Attaining this position is a very elevated status indeed, and it indicates the greatness of Abraham.

a. Abraham's Birth and Childhood

Abraham was a great prophet who lived around 4,000 years ago. The information related in the Qur'an and hadiths does not go into detail. Thus, not all of the information we relay here is verified.

Abraham lived in the period dating from 2200 to 2000 B.C. Some sources say his year of birth was 2000 B.C. There are different oral traditions about his place of birth, but the places mentioned in different sources mostly indicate the vicinity of modern-day Iraq. Some sources say that Abraham's birthplace was Harran, which is forty-five kilometers from Urfa. According to oral tradition, Harran is where Abraham's father lived. According to Tabari, the city of Harran was established by Abraham's brother Haran, the father of Lot. There is no clear information about the birthplace of Abraham in Islamic sources. According to the Old Testament, the birthplace of Abraham is the Chaldean town of Ur; he later left Ur and came to Harran. Today, the city of Ur is in north Iraq.

There is a widespread belief in Urfa, dating back hundreds of years, that Abraham was born in this region. If we accept that Abraham lived 4,000 years ago, it is pointless to make claims about this period when there were no written records. The places where Abraham is said to have lived are all in this region, thus, it is quite likely he was born in Urfa. Some sources state that Abraham visited Urfa during his migration. It is also possible that Abraham may have visited Urfa later and this could have been where he was thrown into the fire.

In the Qur'an it is stated that Abraham's father was called Azar. Another name is said to be Tareh. Azar is thought to have been a vizier of Nimrod. Abraham's mother's name is sometimes given as Nuna, and in some sources it is Ernder binti Nemr. Other traditions state her name either as Usa or Nemre.

During Abraham's lifetime the Babylonians believed that celestial bodies were gods. People used to worship idols in the shape of human beings that represented these celestial bodies. Prophet Abraham fought against this belief system. He explained to people in the clearest possible way that the celestial bodies they worshiped could not be gods. This is related in the Qur'an in the following way:

When the night overspread over him, he saw a star; and he exclaimed: "This is my Lord, (is it)?" But when it set (sank from sight), he said: "I love not the things that set." And when (on another night), he beheld the full moon rising in splendor, he said: "This is my Lord, (is it)?" But when it set, he said: "Unless my Lord guided me, I would surely be among the people gone astray." Then, when he beheld the sun rising in all its splendor, he said: "This is my Lord, (is it)? This one is the greatest of all!" But when it set, he said: "O my people! Surely I am free from your association of partners with God and from whatever you associate with Him as partners. I have turned my face (my whole being) with pure faith and submission to the One Who has originated the heavens and the earth each with particular features, and I am not one of those associating partners with God." His people set out to remonstrate with him. Abraham said: "Do you remonstrate with me concerning God, when He has guided me? I do not fear those that you associate with Him as partners

(and that cannot even benefit or harm themselves, so what do I have to fear of your threats?). Whatever my Lord wills happens, and no evil befalls me unless He so wills. My Lord embraces all things in His Knowledge. Will you not, then, reflect and take heed? (An'am 6:76–80).

In the second station of the Seventeenth Word (The Words), Said Nursi comments about the verse: But when it set, he said: "I love not the things that set" (6:76) as follows:

"A beloved who disappears is not beautiful, for one doomed to decline cannot be truly beautiful. It is not, and should not be, loved in the heart, for the heart is created for eternal love and mirrors the Eternally-Besought-of-All. A desired one doomed to disappear is unworthy of the heart's attachment or the mind's preoccupation. It cannot be the object of desire, and is unworthy of being missed. So why should the heart adore and be attached to it?

I do not seek or desire anything mortal, for I am myself mortal. I do not invoke or seek refuge with something that will decay, for I am infinitely needy and impotent. That which is powerless cannot cure my endless pain or solve my infinitely deep wounds. How can anything subject to decay be an object of worship? A mind obsessed with appearance wails upon seeing that which it adores begin to decay, while the spirit, which seeks an eternal beloved, also wails, saying: 'I love not the things that set.'"

b. Abraham is Thrown into the Fire

Prophet Abraham fought against paganism and he invited people to believe in the oneness of God. He explained to the people that idols were of no benefit either to themselves or to the people who worshipped them. One spring day, everyone left the town for a celebration. Abraham did not join in the celebrations but stayed in town, saying he was feeling ill. He then went to the temple and destroyed all the idols except the largest one. Abraham then hung his ax around the neck of the largest idol. When the people returned, they suspected that Abraham had destroyed the idols and they interrogated him. This incident is related in the Qur'an (Anbiya 21:52–67).

Abraham tried to explain to his people that the real god was not the idols they were worshipping but God who had created the universe. Upon this, Nimrod had Abraham arrested and thrown into a great fire. It is said that Abraham was sixteen at the time. The Qur'an relates this event in the following manner: "They said: Burn him and help your gods, if you are going to do (anything). We said: O fire! be a comfort and peace to Abraham" (21:68–69). Rather than falling into a fire, Abraham fell into a rose garden. When the fire was extinguished, the people came to see Abraham. They found him sitting with a man. Abraham's head was cradled by this man, and he was wiping the sweat off Abraham's forehead. It is believed that this man was an angel. The people then brought Abraham to Nimrod.

According to popular oral tradition, the fire turned into water and the logs into fish. The lake and the fish that formed where Abraham was thrown are considered to be holy today, and visitors from around the world come to see it. However, there is no evidence in the Qur'an or the hadith of the formation of such a lake; rather, it remains a popular belief.

In some accounts Abraham came to Harran after being thrown into the fire and stayed there for fifteen years; thus the blessed land spoken of here could be Harran, but other commentators hold that this land is Palestine.

c. Abraham's Travels

After being thrown into the fire and emerging unscathed, Abraham migrated. He stayed in Harran for a while. Harran is also known as "Abraham's City." Some sources say that a house and mosque belonging to Abraham were in Harran.

After leaving Harran, Abraham arrived in what is today the Akçakale district. Here he married Sarah. There is a water spring at the place where they were married. Today, this spring is known as the "Wedding Spring."

d. Abraham's Death

It is narrated that Prophet Abraham lived for 200 years and passed away in Palestine. Although the exact place of his grave is not known, it is believed that he is buried in the city of al-Khalil, or Hebron, in the cave known by his name.

2. Prophet Job (Ayyub)

Job was a descendant of Isaac, the son of Abraham. His mother was the daughter of Lot, and his wife was the daughter of Mensha, the son of Joseph and the grandson of Jacob. It is said that Job was born south of Palestine. Some sources say that he was born in the Damascus region. According to historians such as Tabari, at the time the Damascus region was a vast area that included the environs of Urfa. Thus, it is possible that Job lived in or around Urfa. It is also said that Job was sent as prophet to Harran and its environs.

Job possessed a great deal of land. He had many sheep and cows, as well as many children. Apart from being very rich, he was also a philanthropist. He helped the poor, fed the needy, and looked after orphans.

Job prayed a great deal and was always thankful for what he had. He is described in the Qur'an as follows:

"Surely We found him full of patience and constancy. How excellent a servant! He was surely one ever-turning to God in penitence" (38: 44). Job is recognized as a prophet of great patience. He invited his people to believe in God, but only seven followed him.

Job suffered a great deal. It is not possible to understand the full scale of his suffering. As Prophet Muhammad said, it is the Prophets who are the most subjected to suffering. It may well be that Job was the prophet who suffered the most. In oral traditions, his sufferings are explained with references to the devil; however this explanation has no basis in the Qur'an and such explanations are not in keeping with the principle of the omnipotence of God.

The general story of Job is as follows:

Job was a man who owned a vast quantity of land and many animals. First he lost all of his possessions. Some were burnt and some of his animals died. He had nothing left. However, nothing changed in Job's life when it came to prayers and obedience to God; he remained thankful to his Lord. Then God tested him with his children. All his children died. Job wept when this happened; however he did not rebel against God, but rather accepted his fate, saying, "It is God who gives and God who takes." Then God tested him with his own life. He became very ill. He had a number of sores over his body, which got worse every day. His wife Rahime never left him and always served him. Despite his illnesses he did not give up his prayers and he kept praising and thanking God.

Not only did he not complain about his sores and afflictions, he did not pray for them to be cured either. He accepted what had befallen him as a token of his submission. Although this state continued for many years, he was patient. Only when it became impossible for him to perform his prayers and recite the name of God, did he pray that he would be cured. Due to his patience in the face of such suffering, he is known as the hero of patience among all people. Bediüzzaman Said Nursi described Job in the following way:

"The prayer of Prophet Job (upon him be peace), the hero of patience, has proved effective as a means of recovery to many who have recited it during their tribulations. However, drawing on the verse, we should say in our prayer: "Truly, affliction has visited me; and You are the Most Merciful of the merciful.""

What follows is a summary of the well-known experience of Prophet Job, upon him be peace.

Job was afflicted with numerous wounds and sores over a long period time, yet he endured his sickness with the utmost patience, thinking that a great recompense would be given in return. But later, when he felt he could no longer worship God with his heart and tongue, which are the seat of knowledge and remembrance of God, he feared that his duty of worship would suffer, and so he said in a prayer, not for the sake of his own comfort, but for the sake of his worship of God: "Affliction has visited me, and You are the Most Merciful of the merciful!" God Almighty accept-ed this sincere, selfless, and devout supplication in the most miraculous fashion. He granted Job perfect good health and made manifest in him a wealth of compassion."

Upon his prayer God gave Job water to wash himself and to drink. He drank from the water and washed himself. Then his wounds were cured. This is described in the Qur'an:

"Strike the ground with your foot: here is cool water to wash with and to drink." We granted him, his household and the like thereof along with them as a mercy from Us, and as a reminder (with guidance and instruction) for the people of discernment. (Sad 38: 42–43)

As is indicated in the verse, after Job regained his health, he also recovered his possessions and his friends and the members of his family who had been estranged from him.

Today, it is believed that the cave in which Job suffered and the water from which he regained his health are situated in the Eyüp district of Urfa. Today, there is a maqam for the Prophet Job here; the cave is here, along with the well that contains the curative water.

There is also a tomb of Prophet Job in the Eyyub Nebi Village of the Viranşehir district of Urfa. The village is twenty kilometers (twelve miles) from Viranşehir. This village is a village of prophets, with shrines to Prophet Job, his wife Rahime and the shrine of Prophet Elisha. However, it must be stated that the places connected to Prophet Job cannot be verified. But the large number of places connected to Prophet Job in this area must account for something.

3. PROPHET ELISHA

E lisha was one of the greatest prophets from the children of Israel. His lineage can be traced back to Prophet Joseph, and thus to Abraham. Some sources say that he was born in 850 B.C., while other sources say that he was born in 726 B.C. It is said that he lived by the River Jordan. Elisha was educated by Elijah for a while. Elisha was a prophet in the region of Damascus and Palestine.

Towards the end of his life Elisha went to visit Job. He searched for Job for years until one day he arrived at a place that was near where Job lived; however, Elisha was not aware of his proximity. By this time he was very old, and he prayed to God to take his soul. Thus, Elijah died without having met Job; it is thought that he died near what is today the village of Eyyub Nebi.

4. PROPHET SHUAYB

I n the Qur'an (Shuara) it is stated that Shuayb was sent to the people of Ayka. Some people say that the people of Ayka were the people of Midian, a region thought to be north of the Red Sea. Thus, we can say that Shuayb was a prophet who was sent to the Arabs. Shuayb is known as "the orator of the Prophets" because of his eloquence. It is believed that the Prophet Shuayb lived in the ancient city which is known as "Şuayb Şehri," located eighty-five kilometers (fifty-three miles) east of Urfa. This town is quite large and is surrounded by city walls. There are rock tombs and a cave that is thought to have belonged to Shuayb in the town. This cave-house is visited today as his maqam.

5. PROPHET MOSES

A fter killing a man and fleeing from Egypt, Moses arrived at the town where Shuayb lived. When he saw two girls come to a well to water their sheep he went to help them. These were the daughters of Shuayb. The girls took him to their father, who asked Moses to stay with them for a while and work for him. Moses worked there for ten years, and then Shuayb gave him one of his daughters in marriage. Moses then returned to Egypt with his wife.

It is believed that the well where Moses met Shuayb's daughters is the well in Soğmatar, sixteen kilometers (ten miles) from the Şuayb Şehri. It is also believed that Moses received his miraculous staff here from Shuayb.

Among the ruins of Soğmatar, which today is known as Yağmurlu Village, there is a well that is thought to be the Well of Moses.

6. PROPHET LOT

According to one account, Lot was the son of Haran, who was either the uncle or brother of Abraham. Lot is believed to have stayed in Urfa with Abraham and to have witnessed him being thrown into the fire. It is also said that he lived in Harran with Abraham and then migrated with Abraham, going to Sodom, where he later became a prophet.

7. PROPHET JACOB

Jacob was the son of Isaac and the grandson of Abraham. After Isaac died, Jacob's mother told him that he had uncles in Harran and that he should go find them, as this was his father's will. Jacob, who was living in Palestine, then migrated to Harran. In Harran he met his uncle's daughter Rachel at a well. He then went to his uncle's house and stayed with him for a while. Jacob told his uncle that he wanted to marry Rachel, but his uncle said that Rachel was the younger sister, and that according to tradition it was not right that the younger sister should be married before the older. Thus, he gave Jacob his older daughter in marriage in return for working for him for seven years. At the end of the seven years he said he would give him Rachel in marriage, but in return Jacob would have to work for another seven years. His uncle loved Jacob very much and wanted to keep him by his side for as long as possible. Jacob had ten sons with his first wife, and Joseph and Benjamin were Rachel's sons. Jacob received revelations and invited people to believe in God and His Oneness.

Jacob's wealth grew and his animals multiplied. After staying in Harran for many years he wanted to go back to Canaan, to Palestine, his homeland. He migrated to Palestine with his family. According to this account, Joseph was born in Harran. Today, the well where Jacob met Rachel in Harran is situated north of the Tomb of Hayat al-Harrani.

B. OTHER IMPORTANT PERSONAGES WHO LIVED IN HARRAN
1. THE POET NABİ

The poet Nabi, who is known as one of the greatest names in Divan literature, is a direct descendent of Prophet Muhammad. His exact date of birth is not known, but it is believed to be either 1640 or 1642. Born in Urfa, he became known as the "Melik al-Shuara," the King of Poets. He made an important name for himself in Divan literature during Ottoman times with his poems. He settled in Aleppo in 1680, and then he was appointed as Istanbul Head Accountant. He died in Istanbul in 1712.

2. SHEIKH MESUD

Sheikh Mesud was one of Ahmed Yesevi's students and he played a great role in the Islamization and Turkification of Anatolia. When the Ayyubids started to rule Urfa in 1182, he came to Urfa with his students from the city of Nishabour near Turkistan.

Then they built a madrasa and a zaviye here. This is the oldest of the tombs in Urfa. It has four iwan classrooms built in the style of Seljuk madrasas. In these four classrooms, four different Islamic schools of thought, or madhab, were taught. The students used to stay in the caves to the southeast of the classrooms. Sheikh Mesud educated many students here, and contributed greatly to the spread of Islam in Anatolia.

3. SHEIKH DEDE OSMAN AVNİ

Sheikh Dede Osman Avni was a great Sufi master of the Qadiri order. He was a descendent of Prophet Muhammad. His exact date of birth is unknown, but he died in 1883. His tomb is in the courtyard of the Mevlid-i Halil Mosque. His is the first tomb there.

4. HACI HAFIZ MUSTAFA EFENDİ

Hacı Mustafa Efendi was one of the greatest scholars of his time and he is buried in the graveyard of the Halilü'r-Rahman Mosque. His date of birth is not known, but he died in 1908. He was a teacher at the Halilü'r-Rahman madrasa, where he taught many students. He taught Miftahizade Hasan Açanal Efendi and Abbas Vasık Efendi.

5. ABBAS VASIK EFENDİ

Abbas Vasık Efendi was also a great scholar of this time. He was born in 1859 in Urfa. He was educated by Hacı Mustafa Efendi in the Halilü'r-Rahman madrasa. He then became a teacher at the same insti-

tution. He specialized in Arabic and religious sciences, and he also spoke good Persian and French, as well as studying physics and mathematics. He worked as a preacher in Iraq for eleven years. Then, in 1908 he was posted as a judge to Harran. In 1913 he was appointed as the mufti of Suruç. He died in 1922.

6. ABDURRAHMAN EFENDİ

Abdurrahman Efendi was one of the greatest scholars and Sufis of his time. He was of the Naqshbandi order. He was originally from Kirkuk and this is where he received his education. He had a spiritual calling to go and serve the people in Urfa. He acted as a spiritual guide to many in Urfa. He appointed Hafız Sheikh Müslüm Efendi as his successor. He died in 1932 and was buried in the Bediüzzaman graveyard.

7. MİFTAHİZADE HASAN AÇANAL EFENDİ

Hasan Açanal Efendi was mufti in Urfa and he was one of the greatest scholars of his time. He was born in Urfa in 1873. He received lessons from Hacı Mustafa Efendi. Apart from the religious sciences, he was also educated in the natural sciences. He spoke Arabic and French. He was a teacher at the Rahimiye Madrasa and became a member of the Urfa Bidayet Court in 1909. He became mufti of Urfa in 1911 but continued to teach. Hasan Açanal Efendi was one of the figures who led Urfa into the National Defense Movement during the War of Independence. He contributed greatly to the liberation of Urfa and received the "Decoration of Liberty."

8. SHEIKH MÜSLÜM HAFIZ

Sheikh Müslüm Hafız was one of the great scholars who made advances in sciences and Sufism. He was of the Naqshbandi order and he was successor to Abdurrahman Efendi. He was imam of Hasan Padişah Mosque. He undertook the restoration and organization of many mosques in Urfa.

It was Sheikh Müslüm Hafız who first constructed the burial place of the great scholar Bediüzzaman Said Nursi in Urfa. Immediately across from the cave where Abraham was born, Sheikh Müslüm Hafız had a two-domed tomb built with two sections. The people were surprised to see that Sheikh Müslüm had had such a tomb built, thinking he had done it for himself. He assured the public: "I did not have these places built for myself. They have two owners. One of them will come from the east and the other from the west and will be buried here." Sheikh Müslüm made this statement but he did not say who would be buried there. When Bediüzzaman Said Nursi died he was buried here. The second place is still empty and waiting for its rightful owner.

9. BULUNTU HACI ABDURRAHMAN EFENDİ

Hacı Abdurrahman Efendi was born in 1865, and was one of the greatest scholars of his time. He became famous as Buluntu Hoca among the public and he was a teacher for many years at the Halilü'r-Rahman madrasa. He was the student of Hacı Mustafa Efendi. He died in 1968, aged 103. His tomb is in the graveyard of the Halilü'r-Rahman mosque.

10. HACI ABDÜLHAMİD EFENDİ (MOLLA HAMİD)

Known as Molla Hamid, Abdülhamid Efendi was a great scholar and Sufi master. He was originally from Bingöl, born there in 1892. He later came to Urfa and stayed here for many years. He took classes from Buluntu Hoca. Later he took lessons from Sheikh Said Efendi in Cizre, and became the master of the Naqshbandi order. He was a teacher for many years in Urfa where he taught many students. He died in 1973 in Urfa. He is buried in the Bediüzzaman Graveyard.

Bediüzzaman said the following about Molla Hamid: "There are two scholars I love best in the world. They are both called Abdülhamid. One of them is from Bingöl, and the other from Urfa." The person buried here is the one Bediüzzaman referred to as Molla Abdülhamid from Urfa.

11. BEDİÜZZAMAN SAİD NURSİ

The great scholar and thinker Bediüzzaman Said Nursi (1877–1960) spent his final days in Urfa.

His greatest goal at the time was to open a modern madrasa in Van. Bediüzzaman believed that one of the

Bediüzzaman Said Nursi

main reasons why the Islamic world had been left behind the times was ignorance, and he believed that this could be solved through education. In the university that he dreamed of, natural sciences would be taught along with religious sciences, and thus a balance of mind and heart would be maintained. Just like the two wings of a bird, these two aspects were to be brought together in mankind. When one is lacking, human beings cannot take flight, they cannot reach their target. He expressed this idea many times at different gatherings but the troublesome years that the country was going through prevented him from putting his project into practice. In March 1960, he came to Urfa, the blessed city he loved so much, and passed away after a few days. Thousands of people attended his funeral at Ulu Cami.

Bediüzzaman Said Nursi's Funeral

FOOD AND ACCOMMODATION

CEVAHİR GUESTHOUSE

Phone: (414) 2159377 / (414) 2161155
Address: Büyük Yol Caddesi
Selahattin Eyyubi Camii Karşısı
Merkez/Şanlıurfa

GÜLHAN RESTAURANT

Phone: (414) 3133318
Address: Atatürk Bulvarı Akbank Bitişiği
Merkez/ Şanlıurfa

ŞANMARAN SHOPPING MALL

Phone: (414) 3163823 / (414) 3163824
Address: Mehmet Akif Ersoy Caddesi
Merkez / Şanlıurfa

HOTEL ERUHA

Phone: (414) 2154411 / (414) 2159988
Address: Balıklıgöl Karşısı Merkez / Şanlıurfa

KİLİM HOTEL

Phone: (414) 3139090 414 3160063
Address: Atatürk Bulvarı Şube Sokak
Merkez / Şanlıurfa

KOÇ OĞLU RESTAURANT

Phone: (414) 3160034
Address: Bahçeli Evler 2. Sk.Yeni
İpek Apt. Altı No:35 Merkez/Şanlıurfa

ÇARDAKLI VILLA

Phone: (414) 2171080
Address: Balıklıgöl Karşısı Merkez / Şanlıurfa

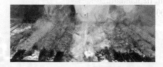

DİVAN PATISSERIE

Phone: (414) 3133540
Address: Emniyet Caddesi Figen Apt. Altı No:30
Merkez/Şanlıurfa

URFA RESTAURANT

Phone: (414) 3156130
Address: Karakoyun İş Merkezi No:226
Merkez / Şanlıurfa

ALTINŞİŞ RESTAURANT

Phone: (414) 2154646 / (414) 2160506
Address: Sarayönü Caddesi Köprübaşı Dünya
Hastanesi Karşısı No:140 Merkez/Şanlıurfa

BİRLİK PATISSERIE

Phone: (414) 2152820
Address: Sarayönu Caddesi No:72/B
Merkez / Şanlıurfa

NT BOOKSHOP/STATIONERY/NEWSAGENT

Phone: (414) 2163460 / (414) 2163489
Address: Atatürk Bulvarı Dünya Hastahanesi
Teknoloji-Kaset Karşısı No:72/A
Merkez/Şanlıurfa

BIBLIOGRAPHY

Açanal, Hasan. Urfa Tarihi, Ankara: Şurkav Yayınları, 1997.

Atasoy, İhsan. Peygamberler Tarihi, İstanbul: Nesil Yayınları, 2006.

Canan, İbrahim. Hz İbrahim'den Mesajlar, İstanbul: Işık Yayınları, 2004.

Cevdet Paşa, Ahmet. Kısas-ı Enbiya Ve Tevarih-i Hulefa, İstanbul: Bedir Yayınevi, 1981.

Cumhuriyetimizin 75. Yılında Birecik, Governorship of Birecik:1998.

Demircan, Adnan. "Hz. İbrahim'in Memleketi Üzerine Bazı Düşünceler", Seyir, No. 11–12, Şanlıurfa: 2005, pp. 39–44.

Düzen, İbrahim. "Hayat B. Kays El-Harrani Hazretleri", Hz. İbrahim (A.S.)'ı Anma Şanlıurfa 1. Kültür Ve Sanat Haftası Faaliyetleri, Edited by Sabri Kürkçüoğlu, Şanlıurfa: Şurkav Yayınları, 1992, pp.109–117.

Elmalı, Abdurrahman. "Şanlıurfa'da Yaşamış Peygamberlerin Kur'ân-ı Kerim'de Geçen Kıssaları", Hz. İbrahim (A.S.)'ı Anma Şanlıurfa 1. Kültür Ve Sanat Haftası Faaliyetleri, Edited by Sabri Kürkçüoğlu, Şanlıurfa: Şurkav Yayınları, 1992, pp.117–124.

Ertan, M. Emin. Hz. İbrahim Ve Nemrut, Ankara: Şurkav Yayınları, 1999.

Fırat, Kerim. Urfa Kahramanları, Gaziantep: 1994.

Güler, Selahaddin E. Urfa Tarihi, Şanlıurfa: Şanlıurfa Dershanesi, 2004.

Her Yönüyle Şanlıurfa 97 İl Yıllığı, Şanlıurfa: Governorship of Urfa, 1997.

İbn Kathir, Abu al-Fida. Al-Bidaya Wa al-Nihaya, Dar al-Kutub al-Ilmiyya, Beirut.

Kandemir, M. Yaşar. "Cabir b. Abdullah," İslâm Ansiklopedisi, Vol. VI, İstanbul: TDV, 1992.

Köksal, M. Asım. Peygamberler Tarihi, Vol I–II, Ankara: TDV, 2004.

Kürkçüoğlu, A. Cihat. Birecik, Ankara: Kültür Bakanlığı, 1996.

———. **Şanlı-Urfa'da Canlanan Tarih,** Şanlıurfa: Şurkav Yayınları, 1995.

Kürkçüoğlu, A. Cihat, Zuhal Karahan Kara. Harran Medeniyetler Kavşağı, Şanlıurfa: Harran Kaymakamlığı, 2003.

Kürkçüoğlu, A. Cihat, Müslüm Akalın, S. Sabri Kürkçüoğlu, Selahattin Güler. Şanlıurfa Uygarlığın Doğduğu Şehir, Şanlıurfa: Şurkav Yayınları, 2002.

Kürkçüoğlu, Sabri. Hz. İbrahim (A.S.)'i Anma Şanlıurfa 1. Kültür Ve Sanat Haftasi Faaliyetleri, Şanlıurfa: Şurkav Yayınları, 1992.

Maraş, Mehmet Atilla. Peygamberler Şehri Şanlıurfa, Şanlıurfa: Şanlıurfa Belediyesi, 1997.

Nursi, Bediüzzaman Said. Lem' alar, İstanbul: Işık Yayınları, 2003.

———. **Bediüzzaman Said Nursi Tarihçe-i Hayatı,** İstanbul: Yeni Asya Neşriyat, 2001.

Oymak, Mehmet. Urfa Ve Hz. Eyyub, Şanlıurfa: Harran Yayınları, 1994.

Öztürk, İbrahim. Sabır Kahramanı Eyyüb Peygamber Ve Şanlıurfa, Şanlıurfa: Elif Matbaası.

Sarıkavak, Kazım. Düşünce Tarihinde Urfa Ve Harran, Ankara: TDV, 1997.

Suman, M. Siraç. Hz. Eyyüb- Hz. Elyesa, Şanlıurfa: Eyyübnebi Beldesi Koruma Derneği.

Şerifoğlu, İsmail. Hayat El-Harrani, İstanbul: Işık Yayınları, 2005.

Şerifoğlu, İsmail. Bediüzzaman'ın Urfa Günleri, İstanbul: Şahdamar Yayınları, 2005.

Şeşen, Ramazan. Harran Tarihi, Ankara: TDV, 1993.

Urfa Hakkında Salname 1927, Translated by Kemal Kapaklı, Şanlıurfa: Şurkav Yayınları, 1998.

Yıldırım, Suat; Kur'ân-ı Hâkim Ve Açıklamalı Meali, Işık Yayınları, İstanbul, 2004.

Yıldız, A. Selami; Şanlıurfa'da Enbiya Kıssaları, Şurkav Yayınları, Şanlıurfa, 2000.